ROYAL LAKE

OVER: Virginia Water in autumn. Anglers near Five Arch Bridge.
(BT)

ROYAL LAKE

The Story of
Virginia Water

by

Raymond South

BARRACUDA BOOKS LIMITED
BUCKINGHAM, ENGLAND
MCMLXXXIII

PUBLISHED BY BARRACUDA BOOKS LIMITED
BUCKINGHAM, ENGLAND

MONOCHROME PRINTED BY
NENE LITHO, WELLINGBOROUGH, ENGLAND
COLOUR PLATES AND JACKET
PRODUCED BY
CHENEY & SONS LIMITED
BANBURY, OXON

BOUND BY
WOOLNOUGH BOOKBINDING
WELLINGBOROUGH, ENGLAND

MONOCHROME LITHOGRAPHY BY
BICESTER PHOTO LITHO LIMITED
BICESTER, ENGLAND

DISPLAY SET IN GOUDY
AND TEXT SET IN GOUDY 11/12pt
BY HARPER PHOTOTYPESETTERS LIMITED
NORTHAMPTON, ENGLAND

Contents

ISBN 0 86023 141 0

Acknowledgements

It is my privilege to acknowledge the gracious permission of Her Majesty The Queen for the use of material from the Royal Archives. I owe a special debt of gratitude for help in my research in the Royal Library to Sir Robin Mackworth-Young, the Royal Librarian, Miss Jane Langton, the Registrar of the Archives, and the Hon Mrs Jane Roberts, Curator of the Print Room.

I have received encouragement and assistance from Mr R. Wiseman, Deputy Ranger of Windsor Great Park, and Mr John Bond, Keeper of the Gardens.

Among the many friends who have helped me in various ways, I would like to thank in particular Daphne Fido for the sketch-maps, and Gordon Langsbury FRPS and Dr Barbara Thompson for their generous help with the colour illustrations.

I am indebted to Mr S.A. Oliver of Egham for information relevant to the origin of the name of Virginia Water and to the extension of the lake at the end of the 18th century.

I am again pleased to acknowledge the help of local libraries, societies and individuals in publicising the book.

Last but not least, I record my thanks, for the fourth time, to Clive Birch and his staff at Barracuda Books for providing me with the opportunity of publishing a fascinating story.

For my grandchildren
John and Gillian Newman
Ruth and Bridget Whitelaw

Preface

Since I first came to Windsor in 1930 I have had an increasing affection for Windsor Great Park and its lakes. My interest in the natural history of the Park grew slowly, but, especially from 1949, when I undertook responsibility for the wildfowl and other surveys, I found myself absorbed in observing and recording the birds.

My last four books have all been chiefly concerned with local history. Here I have had the opportunity of bringing together both history and natural history. I have not attempted a comprehensive account. I hope that some future historian will write a more complete record of the Park, with its wide-ranging interest and importance. The story of Virginia Water is merely one particularly well-documented story within a broader canvas. Even here there are gaps and uncertainties of interpretation, for example over the origin of the name *Virginia* or of the exact part played in its development by Thomas and Paul Sandby. Similarly, I have not tried to be comprehensive in my treatment of the natural history. If the chapters on the Valley Garden and the Birds of the Lake stimulate interest and lead readers to set out to discover more for themselves of the Park's flora and fauna, that will be my reward.

Inevitably in recent years the pressures on Virginia Water have mounted. Its proximity to London and to many other towns has resulted in an ever-increasing number of visitors, especially at week-ends. Those who come in their thousands to Virginia Water and the Valley Garden can threaten the very peace and beauty they come to enjoy. The Park authorities have been alive to the dangers and have protected the amenities with every means in their power. Extensive parking facilities for cars have been provided on the perimeter of the Park. Boating and water sports are not permitted on the lake. There is no intrusion of commercial interests. On the other hand, the walker, the jogger, the angler, the horse-rider, the naturalist can enjoy the freedom of the Park, each in his own way. So the lake which in the past catered primarily for the pastimes and pleasures of kings and courtiers today provides for the enjoyment of all.

Windsor
May 1982

A Fairy Scene

'To the contemplative observer, the view of Virginia Water is an object of the most serious reflection, and of reminiscences which carry him back to the days of its glory and its pride, when all that art could accomplish was lavishly expended to render it a fairy scene, such as some great magician would raise by his potent wand, to give to mortals a foretaste of a heavenly paradise'.

R. Huish, Memoirs of George the Fourth, 1830

The New Fashion

All over the country in the mid-eighteenth century landowners were having their gardens and parks landscaped. The making of Virginia Water has to be seen in the context of this movement, which Nikolaus Pevsner has described as 'the greatest single British contribution to the arts'.

Seventeenth century English gardens were formal, with straight lines, geometric patterns, cut-work parterres. Here the inspiration was mainly French. Versailles cast its spell far beyond the bounds of France. With the accession of William and Mary in 1689 Dutch influence led to the widespread use of topiared yew and box.

Now all was changed. Mrs Delany, that fine old lady who became the much-loved friend of George III and Queen Charlotte, wrote of one estate, that of Lord Cornbury near Burford: 'The ground lies most advantageously and is planted with great skill and a great variety of fine trees, some thick wood, some clumps, in short nature and art have done their best to make it beautiful'. She visited Longleat, the residence of the Marquis of Bath, in 1760 and recorded her impressions: 'There is not much alteration in the house', she wrote, 'but the gardens are no more! They are succeeded by a fine lawn, a serpentine river, wooded hills, gravel paths meandering round a shrubbery all modernised by the ingenious Mr Brown'.

'The ingenious Mr Brown' was Lancelot Brown, most famous of all the landscape architects of the eighteenth century, known as 'Capability' Brown, because, so it was said, he was accustomed to speak of a place as having 'capabilities of improvement'. Many of the aristocrats of this most aristocratic age became passionate devotees of the new landscape gardening. Their rivalries often became bitter as they sought to outdo their neighbours in the pursuit of the new fashion. A lighter note was struck by David Garrick, the actor and playwright, who employed Capability Brown in landscaping the gardens of his house beside the Thames at Hampton. In his play *Lethe or Aesop in the Shades* he has a character by the name of Lord Chalkstone. Waiting to be rowed by Charon across the Styx, Lord Chalkstone turns his spy-glass on the Elysian Fields and comments that they are 'laid out most detestably — no taste! No fancy in the whole world! Your river there, whatd'ye call it? Aye, Styx — why, 'tis as straight as Fleet-ditch. You should have given it a serpentine sweep, and sloped the banks of it. The place indeed has fine *capabilities*, but you should clear the wood to the left and clump the trees on the right'.

Capability Brown is the most famous, but he was not the first in the field. The earliest surviving English landscape garden is that at Claremont in Surrey. This was begun by Sir John Vanbrugh and Charles Bridgeman before 1720 and was extended and naturalised by William Kent in the 1730s. It has been restored by the National Trust, so that we can see it with its lake, island with pavilion, grotto, turf amphitheatre, viewpoints and avenues. At Chiswick House, a few miles away, Kent was employed by the Earl of Burlington to create a garden with a meandering stream and irregular paths. Kent's principle, as Horace Walpole put it, was that 'nature abhors a straight line'. One of Kent's protegés was Henry Flitcroft, who was responsible for much of the landscape architecture in Windsor Great Park.

Flitcroft's work in the Park, such as the High Bridge over Virginia Water, the original 'Belvedere' and the Doric Temple on the hill to the south of the 'Great Lake', has mostly disappeared. Much of his landscape architecture at Stourhead in Wiltshire has, however, survived — the grottos, the Pantheon with its portico and dome towering above the lake, the Temples of Flora and Apollo, the ornamental stone bridge with its grass covered walk.

Stourhead is perhaps the gem of eighteenth century landscaped gardens. Many others are scattered around the countryside. Capability Brown alone had a greater or lesser responsibility for landscaping more than two hundred estates. Two of the greatest were Petworth and Blenheim. At the former the parterres and formal terraces gave way to a 'natural' landscape. The stream was dammed to make a serpentine lake, the park planted with clumps of trees, the Pleasure Grounds laid out to the north of the house and 'the Terrasses reduced to fine undulated steps Adorned with Groups of Cedars, Pines etc'. The incomparable view this gave from the main front of the house later inspired some of Turner's finest landscapes, with the deer silhouetted against the setting sun. Brown effected a similar transformation at Blenheim. When Vanbrugh first created the Palace, fashion ruled that everything within sight of the house should be formal and symmetrical. The Great Parterre, nearly half-a-mile long and as wide as the south front of the palace which overlooked it, was the most majestic feature of this setting. This was in the first part of the eighteenth century. In the 1760s Brown swept away the Great Parterre and created the lake with its cascade by damming the waters of the River Glynne. Temples and meandering walks were added, so that the lake and its environment became 'one continued galaxy of charming prospects and diversified scenes'.

The paradox of eighteenth century landscaping is that, however 'natural' it was supposed to appear, with its lakes and its woodland, its valleys and its slopes, it was hardly ever thought complete without the ornamental additions of pseudo-classical bridges, temples, grottoes, statues, urns or 'ruins'. The aristocrats who formed the élite of eighteenth century society were often steeped in the culture of Greece and Rome. Many went on the 'grand tour' and came to know and admire the antiquities of Italy. Two seventeenth century artists who exercised a wide influence were Nicholas Poussin and Claude Lorrain. Both were Frenchmen, but both settled in Rome and their paintings depict an idealised Roman countryside, landscapes with hills, rivers, sea and trees, but with classical statues, temples, ruins as well. This was the combination which, in more domesticated versions, eighteenth century scenic architects tried to transfer to the settings of English countryside and parkland.

The passion for classical adornments is not difficult to explain. But there was a passion too, illustrated at Virginia Water, for Chinese temples, pavilions, pagodas, boats. It was a passion which seems to emerge from a realm of pure fantasy, all the more because there was little direct knowledge until late in the century of what Chinese buildings and boats really looked like. *Chinoiserie* in other words was a European vision of Cathay, a fantasy rather than a reality. The first *chinoiserie* garden building in England was probably the House of Confucius at Kew, constructed about 1745. It was at Kew also that the most well-known of all the *chinoiserie* buildings of the period — the Pagoda — was erected in 1762. Sir William Chambers, who was the architect of the Kew Pagoda and who had visited Canton in the course of his travels, published *A Dissertation on Oriental Gardening* in 1772, but several books had appeared in the previous twenty years. William Halfpenny had already by 1752 published four volumes of *New Designs for Chinese Temples* and in 1757 William Chambers himself published a folio of *Designs of Chinese Buildings, Furniture, Dresses etc*, with a dedication to Augusta, Princess Dowager of Wales, who came to live at Kew.

A lake (or lakes) was almost always the centrepiece of the new landscaping. Water had often been important in the formal garden, but it was imprisoned in geometrically shaped pools and in fountains. Now streams were dammed, low-lying ground was excavated and a lake created. The soil excavated was used to enhance the existing undulations of the ground and create slopes, mounds and valleys, where trees could be planted. The lake normally had an irregular shape, often following the natural contours of the ground. One of the features of Virginia Water which men praised was that the end could never be seen. Pope's lines about Windsor Forest and Park, though written before Virginia Water was first formed in the middle of the century, were still, or perhaps even more appropriate after the lake had come into being:

> 'Here hills and vales, the woodland and the plain,
> Here earth and water seem to strive again;
> Not, chaos-like, together crushed and bruised,
> But, as the world, harmoniously confused;
> Where order in variety we see,
> And where, though all things differ, all agree'.

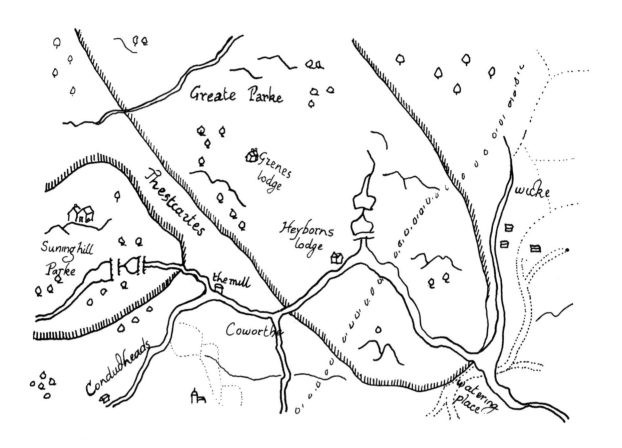

Before the Lake. Detail from John Norden's Map of Windsor Forest, 1607.

Virginia Water in summer. Looking across the arm that leads to Johnson's
Pond towards Virginia Water Cottage and Boathouse. (GL)

ABOVE: View of the Lake. (BT) BELOW. Mandarin and Mallard on
Virginia Water. (GL)

Before the Lake

Virginia Water was thus created in the eighteenth century, during the great age of landscape gardening. The forest streams that made its creation possible had of course been there for many years, probably many centuries. John Norden's maps of Windsor Forest and of the Great Park, two of a series which he made for James I in 1607, show these clearly. Towards the end of his reign James I did in fact spend £600 on 'draining and conveying the water which now overspreadeth divers parts of the great park of Windsor, and maketh it unfruitful'. There is no evidence, however, that the works carried out at that time resulted in the construction of a lake. Norden's maps had shown no more than streams and ponds where Virginia Water now is. Two maps of the mid-eighteenth century — those of John Vardy in 1750 and John Rocque in 1752 — still show nothing more. Within the next few years, however, Virginia Water had come into existence.

In the seventeenth century the Great Park consisted of woods, heathland and swamp. When Samuel Pepys stayed at Cranbourne Lodge in August 1665, he recorded in his *Diary*: 'I walk forth to see the place, and find it to be a very noble seat, in a noble forest, with the noblest prospects towards Windsor and round about over many countys, but otherwise a very melancholy place, and little variety save only trees'.[1]

His *Diary* gives no hint how far to the south of the Great Park (where Virginia Water is now), Pepys went. Yet in fact this southern area, although most remote from Windsor, was one of the earliest parts of the Park. 'The King's Park in the Forest of Windsor' was well named because it was formed by land taken from the Forest and imparked. Much of this southern area had been taken from the Forest by the thirteenth century. Moreover this part of the Park provided a setting for a Royal Manor Lodge. Throughout the Middle Ages Windsor Castle was still primarily a fort rather than a residence. By 1246, in the reign of Henry III, we read of the 'King's houses' and 'the Queen's houses' in the Park and Robert Lightfoot became 'Keeper of the houses in the Park' in 1277. The site of the Manor Lodge was towards the western end of the present Virginia Water, near where in the nineteenth century the Fishing Temple and the Fishing Cottage were situated. For three centuries and more it remained a Royal residence — it was still there at the time of the Commonwealth survey in 1649.

The passion of English kings and their courtiers over the centuries was hunting. Their interest was in the pleasures of the chase, not in the enjoyment of lakes and landscaped gardens. 'He loved the tall stags as if he were their father'. The familiar words which the chronicler applied to William the Conqueror might be applied equally to his successors for the next six hundred years and more.

Until the end of the eighteenth century the Park was more constricted to the south than it is now. The ancient Roman road from London by way of Staines to Silchester ran near its southern boundary, though its exact course in the neighbourhood of the Park is uncertain. To the west, stretches of it are clearly defined and *The Devil's Highway* appears on Ordnance Survey maps. Perhaps this title is of Saxon origin. Just as the Saxons deserted Roman towns like Silchester, so they seem to have had an abhorrence of Roman roads. In mediaeval times the road to London — the forerunner of the present A30 — also touched the southern boundary of the Park. It was conveniently accessible from the King's Manor Lodge and only some five miles to Staines, whence it was possible to proceed to London by river. Thus in 1406 Henry IV, who was lying sick at the Manor, wrote to his Council that he hoped to be well enough to leave Staines for Westminster by water the same evening.

The name of Virginia was already in use in the seventeenth century. There was as yet no lake and hence it was Virginia *River* and this appellation continued until the second half of the eighteenth century. Even in the engravings of the 1750s, when the lake had been formed, the captions still refer to the Virginia *River* and not *Water*. Thus we have: 'View from the North side of the Virginia River, near the Manor Lodge' and 'The Great Bridge over the Virginia River'.

There can be no certainty about the origin of the name. The most obvious derivation perhaps is from Elizabeth, the *Virgin* Queen, whose long and glorious reign had preceded that of the first Stuart. But there is no evidence for this. The colony of *Virginia* does, however, date from the early seventeenth century and could have provided the name, first of the little river, and then of the lake. Later stories which accept the attractively simplistic explanation that the Duke of Cumberland named his lake *Virginia* because he had been Governor of Virginia are completely groundless. For one thing Cumberland was never Governor of Virginia and for another the name of Virginia was in use before Cumberland's time. What we do not know is exactly when and why the name was first applied. G.M. Hughes, in *A History of Windsor Forest, Sunninghill and the Great Park*, published in 1890, records that 'Virginia' is marked on a map of 1662 as the name of a house 'where now stands the under-keeper's lodge' and concludes that the name of the house became the name of the river nearby.[2] That is probably the earliest record of the use of the name in the Great Park. Interesting too is the map of the road from London to Land's End in John Ogilby's *Britannia* of 1675. In the section from Staines to Bagshot the name *New England* occurs where the road skirts Windsor Great Park — near the site of the present Wheatsheaf Inn. *New England Inn* is marked on road maps like those of Daniel Paterson's *Roads of England and Wales* until at least the edition of 1787. The name *Virginia* occurs in place-names in Newfoundland and New Brunswick, both of which had trading links with the colony of Virginia. So the association between the Windsor Great Park names and those of the New World may have some substance. That is probably as far as we can go. And once place-names come into common usage they often remain, and the Virginia River which was there before Cumberland's time became the Virginia Water which he created.

The Manor Lodge was still in use in the Commonwealth period in the 1650s. Bulstrode Whitelocke, who became Constable of the Castle, stayed there and used it to enjoy the hunting in the Great Park, in spite of 'the best stags being all destroyed'. In 1660 Charles II returned to his throne and resumed ownership of the Park. The place of the Manor Lodge as the chief residence in the Park was now taken by Byfield House, a mile to the north. This was named after Captain John Byfield, who had received a grant of land during the Commonwealth and built the new house on it. After the Restoration Charles II took a great interest in the Park. His most enduring memorial is the Long Walk, planted near the end of his reign. Earlier he had re-stocked the Park and Forest with deer and spent much money in improving the Park. Byfield House, or the Great Lodge as it came to be known, was extended and much of the surrounding land was enclosed. Charles, so we are told, used the Great Lodge 'for his own diversion'. A clue to the nature of these diversions may perhaps be found in the association with them of the courtier Baptist May. His biographer says that he 'rendered himself indispensable to the King in his private lodgings . . . and was a frequent and lavish entertainer of the King and his friends'. Pepys dismisses him more summarily as a 'court pimp'. His official position was that of Keeper of the Privy Purse, and he was also from 1671 associated with the Rangership of the Park, although this was not likely to have been more than an honorary position.

Baptist May was succeeded as Ranger by William Bentinck, first Earl of Portland, in 1697. One of the chief supporters of William of Orange, he 'took possession of the Lodge and place of Ranger of

Windsor Park, worth £1500 a year'. He also made extensive alterations to the Lodge and its gardens. He was in Paris in 1698 during the interval between two of the interminable wars between England and France, and had become an admirer of the formal gardens at Versailles.

His tenure of office lasted, however, only five years, and from 1702 to 1746 the Rangership is associated with the Marlboroughs. Sarah Churchill, the future Duchess, had been an intimate friend of Queen Anne before the latter succeeded to the throne. There is a story that Anne and Sarah were once riding together by the Great Lodge, and Sarah said how much she would like to live there for the air. When Anne became Queen in 1702 she granted her wish. 'Anything that is of so much satisfaction as this poor place seems to be to you, I would give Mrs Freeman [her pseudonym for Sarah] for all her days'. At the same time the Queen made Sarah's husband, John Churchill, a KG and Duke of Marlborough. The great victories of the Duke, beginning with Blenheim in 1704, were still to come and he was on the Continent for much of the following years. Sarah, however, made the Lodge her principal residence and both she and her husband spent much of their time here after the wars. Sarah wrote that it was 'of all the places that ever I was in the most agreeable'. The Windsor Great Lodge in fact meant more to the Marlboroughs than the great palace of Blenheim at Woodstock, which was the outcome of the munificent gratitude of the Queen. Sarah said that the Great Lodge was 'a thousand times more agreeable than Blenheim, and I shall pass the greatest part of my life there . . . In a lodge I have everything convenient and without trouble'. The self-willed Duchess always in fact had a love-hate relationship with Blenheim, quarrelling endlessly with the architect, Sir John Vanbrugh, until he left in a rage in 1716. One of the subjects of their dispute was the nature of the ornamental water to be formed, and it was not in fact until the late 1760s that Capability Brown fashioned the great lake at Blenheim, second only to Virginia Water in extent and beauty.

It was at the Great Lodge in 1722 that the Duke of Marlborough died. Sarah carried on the Rangership, living until 1744. Right to the end she continued to be devoted to the Lodge. For the Park as a whole she did not seem to have much affection and there is certainly no hint of any proposals for the kind of improvements associated with the Duke of Cumberland a few years later. She is credited with one comment on the Park that seems an echo of Pepys: 'There is nothing beautiful in it but clumps of trees'. But she also said: 'I never cut down a tree so long as it bear a leaf'. She was obviously, however, more interested in the 'very exact gardens and fountains, cut hedges and groves, pail'd in' than she was in the wilderness of the surrounding parkland.

On her death Sarah left the reversion of the Rangership to her grandson, John Spencer. He died in 1746 and, with the appointment as Ranger of George II's son, William Augustus, Duke of Cumberland, the story of the lakes of the Park begins.

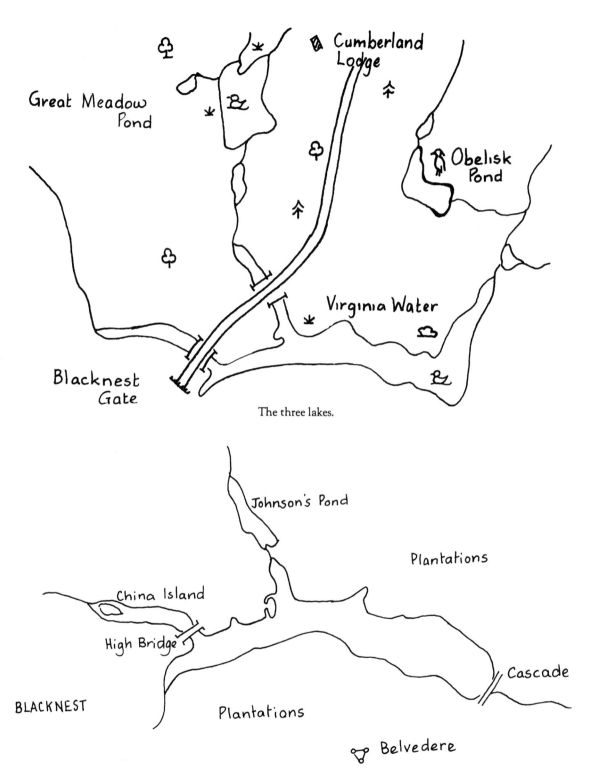

The three lakes.

The First Lake. An approximate outline of the lake formed by the Duke of Cumberland in the 1750s.

A Great Ornament

William, Duke of Cumberland, took up residence at the Lodge as Ranger in the Great Park in October 1746. Only six months earlier he had finally crushed the Jacobite Rebellion by defeating the 'Young Pretender', Bonnie Prince Charlie, at Culloden Moor, near Nairn. The slaughter which followed the battle earned Cumberland the name of 'the Butcher'. History likes to paint portraits in blacks and whites. Perhaps Cumberland was no more the brutal villain than Prince Charles was the romantic hero of tradition. Certainly Cumberland welcomed the life of a country gentleman, when his military duties allowed him the opportunity.

Twice before his death in 1765 his activities as Ranger were interrupted by war. The War of the Austrian Succession, in which Britain was the ally of Austria against France, was still dragging on and William became Commander-in-chief in the Low Countries in 1747. It was not until the Peace of Aix-la-Chapelle in the following year that he was able to return to Windsor and devote himself to the extensive landscaping of the Park associated with his name.

One of the Duke's admirers was Joseph Pote, the Eton bookseller and publisher, whose commercial activities attracted the couplet:

'Jos Pote, a man of great renown,
Buys a book for sixpence, and sells it for a crown'.

More important, he was a local historian who most unusually devoted attention to the Town and the Park as well as the Castle. In his *History and Antiquities of Windsor Castle*, published in 1749, he recorded the appointment of the Duke of Cumberland as Ranger and paid tribute to 'the great and noble improvements now making by his Royal Highness to this Lodge and Gardens'.[1] But he does not mention Virginia Water. This reflects the concentration of the earlier works around the Great Lodge itself. Six years later Pote's *Delices de Windsore* was dedicated to the Duke and described the formation of Virginia Water in glowing terms. 'The noble Piece of Water in the Valley', he wrote, 'was effected at a large expense, and from a small Stream or Current of Water is now made a spacious River capable to carry Barges, and Boats of Pleasure with freedom . . . This Piece of Water is a great Ornament to the Park, and terminates in a Grotto, and large Cascade or Fall of Water, and whilst the Beauties of Nature are thus happily assisted by Art, what may not be expected in a few Years from such noble and extensive Designs, under the Guidance of a munificent and Royal Intendant'.[2] Having scaled the heights of prose he now broke into verse:

'Here blest with Health, with Glory blest,
From military Labour rest —
Till Britain calls — Then leave these Plains
For Victory, and new Campaigns;
Then Public Liberty compleat,
Rebellion quash, and Tyranny defeat'.

These hopes were not realised. The outbreak of the Seven Years War in 1756 led to a resumption of Cumberland's military career. This time, however, the forces under his command were defeated and Cumberland found himself as unpopular as before he had been popular. In disgust he threw up his military appointments and retired to the Great Park once more. His last years were clouded by increasing ailments — a paralytic stroke in 1760, partial blindness, asthma, obesity. When he died in 1765 he was still only 44.

Nonetheless by this time Cumberland had created the first Virginia Water and landscaped the southern part of the Great Park so that, over two hundred years later, it still bears the impress of his initiative and enterprise. Neither George I nor George II had shown much interest either in Windsor or in Windsor Great Park. So Cumberland was free to do pretty much as he pleased. This was the time when, all over England, parks were being re-designed according to the new fashion, with lakes, cascades, landscaped slopes, scenic bridges and temples. The Duke was intimate with several of the aristocratic 'improvers', notably perhaps the fourth Duke of Devonshire, whose Chatsworth estate in Derbyshire was re-modelled.

The most famous of the new landscape gardeners, Capability Brown, does not appear to have been brought in at Windsor. William Kent, one of his predecessors, had done work at Windsor itself in the 1730s, but his work had not extended to the Park and in any case he died in 1748. One of his pupils, however, Henry Flitcroft, as we have seen, did do work for the Duke of Cumberland. He was paid £1,900 on account for work in Windsor Great Park, and his close association with the Duke is illustrated by the dedication to him of a volume of his architectural drawings and designs.

The Cumberland Papers in the Royal Archives at Windsor include a number of lists of trees and flowering shrubs, which show just how much planning and effort went into the planting up of the Park. The first of these records, contained in a small neatly-written notebook, lists 138 flowering shrubs, beginning with Bastard Indigo; the main list is followed by sections on Roses (38 species), Honeysuckles (11 species), Elders (4 species) and Thorns (23 species). Next comes a list of trees, with over 200 entries, beginning with Triple Thorn'd Acacia, Pseudoacacia and Arbor Vitae and proceeding through the whole gamut of the alphabet to Weeping Willows. There is evidence of much correspondence with the Governors and other important persons in the American colonies — Mr Glynne, Governor of South Carolina; Col Francis Willis of Gloucester County in the colony of Virginia; Capt Rutherford and Lewis Morris Esq of New York; Mr Richard Salter of New Jersey; Eliakin Hutchinson, Peter Charndon and Dr William Clarke of Boston; Governor Hamilton, Richard Peters and Mr Bartram of Pennsylvania; Mr Bull and Mr Pinchney, two of His Majesty's Council at Charlestown in South Carolina. The wealth of the flora of the eastern seaboard of what was soon to become the United States is reflected in the lists. A random selection does scant justice to the variety: Broad-leaved Magnolia, 'Ginsery or Ninsain of the Chinese', Philadelphus flore alba, Catalpa Tree, Candleberry Myrtle, Blue-berried Bay, Tulip Tree, White-flowered Azalea, Pyrola, Mezerion, Cytisus, Arbor Jude, Cistus Landifera, Chinquefin Chestnuts . . ., as well as a wide range of Oaks, Planes, Hornbeams, Maples, Poplars and many other trees. There is correspondence about the receipt of seeds from South Carolina at Portsmouth, to be sent to the Bailiff at the Lodge in Windsor Great Park. In 1759 there are records of 'experiments upon cuttings of Different Sorts'. Forest seeds, all carefully labelled, were still being sent in 1760 by Gen Amherst who, before he went to North America, had been on the Duke's staff on the continent.

One list is of seeds brought from the West Indies. Many of the items are described, so that the list reads very much like a nurseryman's catalogue. 'Barbardoes Bachelor Buttons' is 'a little Tree that bears a Red flower like a Button'. The 'Christmas Bush' is 'a little Tree about the size of a Gooseberry that . . . is covered with little white flowers'. The 'French Rose bears a large Rose that is Red in the morning and white in the afternoon'. The 'Bird Pepper grows on a little Green Bush, bears a little Red Berry, and looks very pretty'.[3]

It would be fascinating to know in more detail where the planting was done, how much for example in the vicinity of the Great Lodge itself and how much around Virginia Water, and what was the fate of the flowering shrubs. Some of the original trees are certainly still standing. A marker plaque in the heart of the present Valley Garden has the date 1747 and the cedars in the Avenue that leads from Fort Belvedere to the lake were planted about 1760.

One feature of the planting seems to have been the use of conifers — cedars, scotch firs, pines — as well as the oaks and other hardwoods more traditionally associated with English parkland. A German, Prince Pückler-Muskau, who visited the Park in the 1820s, recorded his surprise at seeing 'the whole country here assume a new character and one very uncommon in England — that of my beloved Fatherland: — fir- and pine-wood intermingled with oaks and alders; and under foot our heather, and even our sand'.

The Great Lodge itself was extended and largely re-built. It still continued to be known by that name, with variations such as Upper Lodge or Windsor Great Lodge. At some time later in the century, however, it was given the name of *Cumberland* Lodge which it still bears today. The contemporary engraving by Thomas and Paul Sandby gives a most attractive view of the large and stately mansion, framed by massive oaks, with the Duke setting forth in his coach drawn by four lively brown horses, and deer *and ostriches* on the lawns at the side of the road. The eighteenth century house no longer exists, but the imposing former stable block, built during the 1750s (it can be seen through the trees in the engraving), remains to witness to the extent of Duke William's alterations.

Cumberland Lodge and Stables in 1754. *Thomas and Paul Sandby.* (RL)

The three lakes — Great Meadow Pond ('the Great Lake'), the Obelisk Pond ('Hurst Lake' was its original name) and Virginia Water — were substantially completed in the period of four years from 1748 to 1752. The preparatory work was on an immense scale. Heathland and scrub had to be cleared. Streams had to be dammed. Swampy land had to be drained and the lakes banked. Hill slopes and valleys had to be fashioned to create a landscaped environment. Trees by the thousand had to be planted — thirteen new plantations of woodland were formed around Virginia Water alone. Lawns had to be laid out; Smith's Lawn, named after Barnard Smith who was the Duke's Groom, was the most extensive. Roads had to be made and fences erected.

Much of the labour for the work in the Park was provided by Cumberland's soldiers. Many were mercenaries of German, especially Hanoverian, origin. It is probable that some of the troops disbanded after Culloden were given work in the Park. Certainly there were many men in the labour force after 1748 who had served in the Duke's regiments. Cumberland himself covered at least the major part of the cost of the undertaking from his privy purse — just as any other great landowner did. Instead of paying higher wages than others, we are told, he ordered the labourers, every day, at noon, table-beer with bread and cheese, besides which he gave them a substantial dinner once a week. A nobleman (or, according to one version of the story, his sister, the Princess Amelia, who kept house for him) took the liberty one day to tell the Duke that His Royal Highness could do very well without so many labourers, who must put him to a prodigious expense. The Duke heard him (or her) out, and then said: 'To be sure, as you say, I might do without these poor people, but can they do without me?'

Lawlessness had been widespread in the Park and Forest in the first part of the eighteenth century. When George I came to the throne, the railing of the Great Park was so rotten that the deer 'daily get out, and are killed by the country people'. The deer pens were in ruins and the surviving deer were at daily risk. Poaching was prevalent and it was said that 'the park is almost become common'.[4] It is necessary perhaps to set Horace Walpole's comment that Cumberland soon 'disgusted the neighbourhood by excluding them from most of the benefits of the Park' in the context of this situation. The exclusion was nonetheless clearly ineffective because, only shortly before Cumberland's death in 1765, a notice was issued that 'Whereas from the Indulgence granted to poor People, to pick up the dead Wood in Windsor Great Park, great inconveniences have been found to be very Prejudicial to the Breed of the Game there . . . no Person . . . do presume to enter into the said Park, and strole about therein, under pretence of Birds Nesting, or any Pretence Whatever'.[5]

Of the three lakes which were the outcome of Cumberland's activity, the 'Great Lake' (the present Great Meadow Pond) and the Obelisk Pond came first. They are both shown on John Rocque's contemporary map. This is dated 1752, but can be assumed to represent the lay-out of the Park a year or two earlier. The *name* of Virginia Water appears, but only the streams which were utilised to form the lake are shown. Probably the construction had been started but not completed. That the two Ponds should come first is natural. Both are much nearer to Cumberland Lodge. The 'Great Lake' lies immediately below the Lodge and was its obvious companion. An eighteenth century print shows smooth lawns sloping down to the lake, where now are fields and reed-beds. A pond is marked on Norden's *View of the Great Park* exactly where the lake was later formed. It is interesting to speculate that its name of Mistle Pond reflected the abundance of mistle thrushes in the Park — they are still among the commoner birds. The name of Mezel Hill, by the present Royal School and near both Cumberland Lodge and Great Meadow Pond, may be a corruption of *mistle*. The excavation of the 'Great Lake' was itself a major work. It is over 30 acres in extent and has survived to become a nature sanctuary, for which purpose its privacy is strictly protected. The main stream that feeds Great Meadow Pond continues by way of Mill Pond and Johnson's Pond to become one of the most important tributaries of Virginia Water.

The Obelisk Pond is a smaller lake but still of substantial size. Although the two Ponds are separated by little more than the expanse of Smith's Lawn, they are different in character. The area of Great Meadow Pond is London clay; that of the Obelisk Pond is the Bagshot sands which are typical of much of the southern part of the Park. Great Meadow Pond is in Berkshire; the Obelisk Pond is in Surrey. Great Meadow Pond is surrounded by reed-beds; the Obelisk Pond is framed by woodland and rhododendrons. The stream which feeds the latter is that which forms such a central feature of the Savill Garden, and it continues at the south-eastern outlet of the Pond to join with another of the tributaries of Virginia Water, reaching the lake by way of Wick Pond.

The soil excavated when the Pond was formed was probably used to increase the height of the hill to the north-east, and here stands the Obelisk which gives its name to the Pond. The inscription on the monument reads: 'This Obelisk was raised by command of King George II, commemorates the services of his son William, Duke of Cumberland, the success of his arms, and the gratitude of his father. This tablet was inscribed by His Majesty King William IV'. The Obelisk forms the focal point of one of the vistas from Cumberland Lodge.

Some of the phases in the early planning of the lakes are obscure. We know that William, Duke of Cumberland, was the grandee who commissioned and financed the works that transformed so much of the Park. However, just how great was the contribution of Henry Flitcroft and others is difficult to assess. For many years it has been the commonly accepted view that Virginia Water was the creation of the artist brothers Thomas and Paul Sandby. This view has been subjected to challenge. Thomas was not, for example, as many accounts suggest, appointed Deputy Ranger of the Park immediately following the Duke's own appointment as Ranger; he probably did not become Deputy Ranger until just before the Duke's death in 1765. He then held that position until his own death in 1798 and during that time lived at the Lower Lodge (where Royal Lodge now is). His administrative responsibilities in the Park must have been extensive; even so the part he personally played in the extension and reconstruction of the lake at the end of the century was limited.

End of the First Lake, showing Cascade, Grotto and Bridge. *Thomas and Paul Sandby.* (RL)

Nevertheless the Sandby brothers occupy an important place in the story. For one thing they had for many years a close association with Duke William. Both were with him on the Scottish campaign. Thomas, the elder, had been born at Nottingham in 1721 and was thus the same age as the Duke. In 1743 he had been appointed his private secretary and draughtsman. After Culloden it is likely that Thomas came to Windsor with the Duke. He went with him to the war in the Netherlands and probably remained there until the conclusion of peace. From 1748 he was at Windsor, sometimes living at Cranbourne Lodge where the Duke himself resided at times, when the Great Lodge was undergoing repairs and re-building. He continued to be described as draughtsman to the Duke; later he became architect and, in 1764, Steward to the Duke.

Thomas's younger brother, Paul, stayed on in Scotland after the suppression of the Jacobite Rebellion, to assist in the military survey of the new line of road to Fort George on the Moray Firth. He was afterwards appointed draughtsman to the survey, and the many prints and drawings he made are witness to his activity. He did not quit the service of the survey until 1751 and it was then that he went to reside for a time in the Park with his brother.

One of the first-fruits of their partnership at Windsor was the *Prospectus* of 1754. Dedicated to the Duke, this consisted of eight folio plates. They were drawn by Thomas and engraved on copper by Paul and 'the best engravers of the day'. We have no comparable series of views of the creation of Virginia Water, the Great Lake and the Belvedere and this in itself gives the Sandbys a special importance. Both the brothers were accomplished artists and became Royal Academicians. Paul excelled as a water-colourist. Over the years — he did not die until 1809 — he travelled widely, depicting any scene or building that took his eye. Above all, the sketches and paintings of the two brothers not only delight the eye but present us with a lively and vivid picture gallery of the Castle, the Town and the Park in their day.

The first Virginia Water was probably the largest single 'artificial' lake created in the country during the mid-eighteenth century period of landscape gardening. It was over one-and-a-half miles in length, extending as far as the dam or 'pond-head' which was constructed roughly on the line between the present Botany Bay Point and the 'Ruins'. The water was thus held back, save where it tumbled over a cascade. The main stream then continued under the London road, which lay immediately to the east. The area between the lake and Smith's Lawn was landscaped and planted with trees and shrubs, while belts of woodland framed the whole development.

Virginia Water was something over and above the ornamental lake which normally formed part of eighteenth century landscaping. Most of the artificial waters of the period were immediately below the great house and in full view from it. This is true of Stourhead, Sheffield Park, Blenheim and many others. At Windsor the 'Great Lake' occupied this position. But here, a mile to the south, was a swampy depression which offered opportunities for the creation of a larger lake, capable of carrying pleasure craft and providing opportunities for architectural adornment and landscaping on the grand scale. Virginia Water fits into the parkland scene so perfectly that it seems as natural as any lake could be. But the original conception was excitingly imaginative.

The passion for *chinoiserie* which was a feature of some of the great works of eighteenth century landscaping has already been mentioned. The first touch of fantasy at the new Virginia Water was the launching of a 'Chinese' yacht, the *Mandarin*. The Sandby brothers have illustrated this for us in several of their drawings. There is first the portrayal of the *Mandarin*, after a voyage up the Thames, being brought ashore at The Bells of Ouseley at Old Windsor. In the representation in the Royal Library at Windsor the hulk — for this is all it was at this stage — is being hauled from the river by a large team of oxen. Buildings and trees, as well as the river itself, are sketched in the background. A much more complete representation is in the Victoria and Albert Museum. The hulk itself is in the same position, but now we have a crowd of spectators, men, women, children, dogs, all obviously enjoying the unusual sight. The Duke of Cumberland himself is now present and his corpulent figure is prominent in front of a large tree. The transport of the vessel from the river to the lake must have presented difficulties. The distance is some three miles and, whatever the route, there was at least the initial hill as well as the problem of traversing roads unaccustomed to such a use.

Presumably the conversion of the hulk into a Chinese yacht or junk took place on Virginia Water itself. Another of the Sandby drawings shows the completed vessel on the lake with all its whimsical finery and trappings. Mrs Delany described how it was 'as rich and gay as carving, gilding and japanning can make it'. Fearsome dragons with flames issuing from their mouths are painted on the sides of the vessel, while the yacht is ornamented with lanterns and bells. In the Sandby drawing the yacht is afloat on the lake, while on the shore is a group of lords and ladies. The Duke of Cumberland is showing the yacht to the King or another member of the Royal family and we are told that, when entertaining his nephew, the future George III, on board, the Duke had the vessel illuminated.

Along with the yacht were two other boats, one of which provided accommodation — on suitable occasions — for a military band. Thomas Arne's *Rule Britannia* had been given its first performance only a few years before, in 1739, in the little amphitheatre at Cliveden, only a few miles upstream from Windsor. Did the Duke step on board his yacht to the stirring strains of its music? Certainly a rich repertoire was available to the band, with Handel's *Water Music* among the obvious choices (but not, presumably, Chinese music). The shores too could have been graced with all the colour and charm of *fêtes champêtres*, but of such we have no record.

At the head of the lake, on what has ever since been known as China Island, a summer house, again in the Chinese style, was erected. A certain Mrs Lybbe Powys was among its admiring visitors. Writing in 1766, she said: 'We went to the Chinese Island, on which is a small house quite in the taste of that nation, the outside of which is white tiles set in red lead, decorated with bells and Chinese ornaments. You approach the building by a Chinese bridge, and in a very hot day, as that was, the whole looked cool and pleasing. The inside consists of two state rooms, a drawing-room and bed-chamber, in miniature each but corresponds with the outside appearance'. Charles Knight, in his *Windsor Guide* of 1793, has a more detailed description. 'The structure is small', he said, 'but elegant and striking; the middle room is of scarlet-green, richly ornamented with gold; the panels of the doors are of looking-glass, which has a pretty effect; the right-hand room has all the necessary conveniences of a kitchen; and the other room, which forms the left wing, is hung with white satin, painted, in which is a settee of the same'.[6]

The hulk of the *Mandarin* being brought ashore at the Bells of Ouseley, Old Windsor, in 1753, for transportation to Virginia Water. *From a gouache by Paul Sandby.* (V & A)

Often the *Mandarin* was moored by China Island, but it frequently took the Duke and his guests for excursions along the whole length of the lake. Half-a-mile or so from China Island it would pass under the 'High Bridge'. This was a wooden bridge, also in 'the Chinese taste', with a single span of 165 feet — said to be the highest in the world and five feet wider than the famous Rialto at Venice. The Sandby painting shows the bridge about where the present Blacknest or Five Arch Bridge is — still called the 'High Bridge' on Ordnance Survey maps. The lake is not wide at this point — indeed the name of Virginia *River* continued to be used and from a number of viewpoints it still resembles a river rather than a lake. A number of labourers are engaged on various tasks, watched by the Duke on horseback. There are wheelbarrows and horse-drawn carts, while on the other side of the lake, beyond the bridge, a line of cows is coming down to drink. The *Mandarin* yacht is in the background, where the arm of the lake reaches back to Johnson's Pond.

Mrs Delany described her impressions on a visit in 1757, when the Duke was away on the Continent. The party walked across the 'desperately steep' High Bridge and recorded that it was so contrived that 'any piece that is decayed may be taken out and repaired without injuring the rest'. They walked across because they were apprehensive about driving, 'though carriages of all sorts go over it every day'.

29

Away on the horizon in the picture of the bridge appears a tall building. This was the triangular Belvedere on Shrubs Hill, almost directly above the eastern end of the lake. Fort Belvedere, in its present much larger form, is now too much enclosed by woodland to be seen from Virginia Water. It is often, however, to be seen in early views of the lake. It illustrates perfectly the use of the word 'belvedere' to describe 'a raised turret (or turrets) from which to view scenery', for from it there were views not only of the lake below but of Windsor Castle to the north, St Paul's Cathedral to the east and the line of the Hogsback away to the south in Surrey. An engraving of the 1750s shows the *Mandarin* moored by the side of the lake, with Shrubs Hill and the Belvedere behind. Other boats are also in the picture, along with several swans. Charles Knight, writing later in the century, said: 'The Belvedere on Shrubs Hill is a triangular building that has a tower at each corner, one of which is a staircase, the other a library and the third a china closet'. Even in this space of time Knight was able to describe it as 'encompassed by a fine plantation of trees'. Most notable was a majestic avenue of cedars leading from the Belvedere to the shores of the lake.

Duke William's death in 1765 at least meant that he did not have to witness the destruction of his lake on the first of September three years later. On that day a storm which arose in the night deluged London and the country around with torrents of rain for eight hours. The *Annual Register* recorded that 'the late Duke of Cumberland's fine water-works in Windsor Forest were entirely destroyed; several persons were drowned in different places, as well as horses, oxen and hogs'. Mrs Delany wrote to a friend: 'I suppose the newspapers have informed you of the extraordinary inundation caused by only one night's rain on Thursday last. The Virginia Water broke head and is entirely gone, fish and all, and a house in its way carried off as clean as if no house had ever been built there'.

Virginia Water, with Chinese yacht. *Thomas and Paul Sandby.* (RL)

The Duke of Cumberland's Chinese Temple, China Island. (RL)

The High Bridge, Virginia Water. *Thomas and Paul Sandby.* (RL)

The Belvedere on Shrubs Hill. *Thomas and Paul Sandby.* (RL)

The Royal Renewal

For over sixty years Windsor was neglected by the Hanoverian kings. Their neglect throws into relief the achievement of William, Duke of Cumberland, in his transformation of the Park. It was not until the years following 1775 that George III began the interest in Windsor which led to the second chapter in the eighteenth century history of the Park. His predecessor, George II, had lived at St James Palace, and sometimes at Kensington and Hampton Court. George III acquired a new house in London (the Queen's House, now incorporated in Buckingham Palace) and used St James only for court ceremonies. He abandoned Kensington and Hampton Court and made Kew, and later Windsor, his country residences.

Queen Charlotte had a hand in bringing the King to Windsor. The Royal family had increased steadily; by 1775 there were ten young princes and princesses. The old rambling Castle itself had, however, a miscellaneous assortment of occupants and so new accommodation was sought. First, the house in the Castle grounds in which Queen Anne had resided was acquired; then, a new barrack-like building which became known as the Queen's or the Upper Lodge as it was called, was purchased by the Queen from the Duke of St Albans.

At first the King intended only to stay at Windsor occasionally but he became more and more attached to it. He disliked London. 'I certainly see as little of London as I possibly can, and am never a volunteer there', he was to say in 1785. He learned to enjoy the country life which Windsor and its Park offered him. The Court was maintained but divested of much of the pomp and ceremonial that was normally associated with it. George was the King but he was also 'the Squire of Windsor' and participated in the life of the town. He involved himself in the parliamentary elections for the borough and even personally canvassed the tradesmen in the interests of his favoured candidates. He was a frequent attender at the local theatre. The younger Charles Knight remembered as a boy seeing the King in his father's bookshop on Castle Hill, 'a quiet good-humoured gentleman in a long blue coat', turning over the publications like any other customer. He took pleasure in watching the boys playing cricket or flying their kites in the park. 'Many a time', wrote Knight, 'had he bidden us good-morning when we were hunting for mushrooms in the early dew and he was returning from his dairy to his 8 o'clock breakfast. Everyone knew that most respectable and amiable of country squires and His Majesty knew everyone'.[1]

Just as the King came to be devoted to Windsor so he came to love the Park. He was fond of hunting; he was fond of riding. The Park was ideal for both. Two other activities came to occupy much of his time and interest. One was the creation of the Royal farms. The other was the restoration and extension of Virginia Water.

Duke William's residence in the Great Park had coincided with the high tide of eighteenth century landscape gardening. George III's residence at Windsor coincided with the high tide of the eighteenth century 'agrarian revolution'. Compact farms, new patterns of crop rotation, the improvement of stock breeding were some of the outstanding features of the new farming. George III led the fashion in his 'model farms' in the Park.

The man responsible for the development of the farms, appointed in 1791, was Nathaniel Kent. As a young man Kent had held a minor diplomatic post in Flanders and had taken a great interest in the husbandry methods of the Flemish people, which he considered to be 'in the highest perfection' in any part of Europe. In this country he was acquainted with the Norfolk system, associated with names like that of Thomas Coke of Holkham, which in his view came 'as near to the practice of the Netherlands as any made use of in England'. He set aside large areas of Windsor Great Park, at the time covered with moss, ferns and rushes and interspersed with bogs and swamps. These were cleared, drained, fenced and then gradually transformed into the two farms, *Flemish Farm* and *Norfolk Farm*. The King, this time in his capacity as 'Farmer George', took a personal interest in Kent's work and Kent responded by keeping a *Journal of the Progressive Improvements in Windsor Great Park* for the information of the King. The *Journal*, written in an exquisite hand and beautifully bound in three volumes, is in the Royal Library at Windsor.

The King often visited the farms. In the spring of 1793 Kent ordered the Windsor steward to 'pay due attention at all leisure time to the Roads, that they may be so formed and mended in the course of the Summer that His Majesty may be able to Visit the Farms next Winter with Safety and Comfort'. On these visits he talked to all and sundry. Once he met a boy in the Park. 'Who are you?', asked the King. 'I be pig boy', replied the lad, 'but I don't work. They don't want lads here. All this belongs hereabouts to Georgy'. 'Pray, who is Georgy?'. 'He be King and lives at the Castle, but he does no good for me'. The King found him a job on one of his farms.

Chronologically, the development of the Royal farms belonged mainly to the 1790s. The creation of the second Virginia Water came earlier. The King's active interest in fact began soon after his coming to Windsor. There were probably repairs to the dam which had been carried away at the time of the storm of 1768, but no major reconstruction took place and there are indications that later storms undid whatever repairs had been attempted. Duke William had been succeeded both as Duke of Cumberland and as Ranger by Henry, the youngest brother of George III. Duke Henry resided from time to time at Cumberland Lodge and continued as Ranger until his death in 1790. It would not be true to say that he took no interest in the Park, but certainly there was none of the active involvement of his uncle, the previous Duke. This is hardly to be wondered at. In 1771 he contracted a clandestine marriage without the King's consent. The King was never reconciled to the marriage and Henry lived for the rest of his life in the shadow of his brother's disapproval. His dependence on the King for financial support did not prevent him from falling deeply into debt and, during the later years of his life, he spent much of his time abroad.

On his death William Frederick, the son of the Duke of Gloucester, nominally became Ranger, but in practice the King himself assumed control. Thomas Sandby continued as Deputy Ranger and lived in the Lower Lodge where he died in 1798. Although it was his practice to spend a part of each year in London, he gave a great deal of his time to the Park. The King gave him his confidence and his personal friendship, not only showing an interest in his activities but frequently visiting him at the Deputy Ranger's Lodge without ceremony or previous announcement. One of Thomas Sandby's daughters used to tell how she and her sisters, on hearing the King calling for her father, stepped out of the window of the room in which they were sitting and ran through the back of the house to change their dresses, before making their appearance at luncheon with His Majesty.

As with the earlier period the extent of Thomas Sandby's personal share in the reconstruction of Virginia Water is open to question. His pencil and brush were constantly at hand to delineate designs and to sketch the various works, and letters illustrating his involvement have been preserved. Responsibility for the administration of the Park was, however, shared between the Crown and Parliament. In 1810 authority was devolved on three Commissioners of Woods, Forests and Land Revenues, the predecessors of the present-day Crown Estate Commissioners. For many years before this there had been two Surveyors-General, one of whom, the Surveyor-General of Woods, Forests, Parks and Chases, was in overall charge of the restoration and

LEFT: View towards the Wick end of the Lake. (BT) RIGHT: The Cascade, not very different from the early 19th Century view. (RS) BELOW: The 'Ruins' at the present time. (RS)

OVER : Azalea Valley in spring. Lysichitums and daffodils; Azalea shrubs to left and right will be a blaze of colour later. (BT)

extension of Virginia Water. It was John Pitt who as Surveyor-General initiated the legislation to purchase additional land from Egham Parish to the east of the Park. An Act was passed in 1782 for this purpose. Its preamble referred to the King's desire to restore 'an ancient piece of water which flows through or over parts of Windsor Great Park the head of which by means of a late flood was broken down'.[2] In the previous November, at a meeting held in the vestry of Egham Parish Church, the parishioners had agreed that around 43 acres on waste Common land on Bagshot Heath could be handed over to the King, in return for three guineas and five guineas being paid annually by the King and his successors for the poor of Egham.

So it was not until 1788 that the way was clear for the reconstruction of Virginia Water to go ahead. There were delays in the negotiations with Egham Parish. Properties had to be acquired and demolished. What remained of the ancient village of Harpesford with its Chapel disappeared beneath the lake. The Great West Road (the present A30) had to be diverted. The extended lake began at what became known as Botany Bay Point. Botany Bay on the coast of New South Wales had been discovered in 1770 in the course of Captain Cook's voyage of discovery and so named by the naturalists of the expedition. What prompted the adoption of the name at Virginia Water is a mystery, but it seems reasonable to associate it with the extension of the lake in which it was a focal point. When the extension was complete there was a broad new expanse of water to the east of the old lake. Where the stream continued its course a grand Cascade had been constructed. From the bank above the Cascade a vista extended far up the lake. To the left, on Shrub's Hill, was the Belvedere. To the right, sweeping round from Botany Bay Point, was a new arm of the lake reaching to the bridge and small cascade which divided the main lake from Wick Pond. The latter was formed by the damming of two streams. The whole of the extension was landscaped and in the course of time surrounded by woodlands.

In the Public Record Office is preserved a bundle of yellowed documents which include much of the correspondence relating to the reconstruction of Virginia Water.[3] Some are damaged by damp; some are frayed and some almost illegible. But they still reach across the two centuries which have elapsed and afford insight into the meticulous care that was taken over the planting of trees and shrubs, as well as every detail of the works themselves. The King's interest is often apparent. Plans were submitted to him and he made frequent visits to view the progress of the works. Thomas Courtenay, the Foreman of the Works, wrote on 19 August 1788 to John Robinson, the new Surveyor-General of Woods and Forests: 'I am happy to inform you that the King, Prince of Wales and Duke of York was here this day and went round all the Works; he Expressed great Satisfaction at what was done since he was here, and gives you the greatest Credit for your Exertions and what has been done since you came into office and all done much to his liking'.

John Robinson, who plays a prominent part in the story, was a Tory minister who became a great favourite of George III not only as a politician, but also as an agriculturist. A northcountryman by background, he had been Secretary of the Treasury under Lord North from 1770 to 1782 and in 1787 had been appointed as Surveyor-General of Woods and Forests. He lived at Wyke Manor at Isleworth, between Brentford and Osterley Park, so that he was in a position to pay frequent visits to Virginia Water, and from the beginning had the oversight of all that went on.

Robinson clearly, subject to the wishes of the King, had the last word on major decisions, but Thomas Sandby was Deputy Ranger and had the advantage of forty years' experience of the Park. He held site meetings with Robinson and wrote many letters to him in which he went into details about his views. He was particularly keen on vistas. 'These Cuts or Vistas', he wrote, 'in my Opinion will contribute to the pleasure in passing thro' that close side, by enlivening it with a greater degree of agreeable Objects, such as Views of that branch of the Virginia River by the Wick and into the Park where there are fine Trees to make a termination'.[4]

The original Cascade also appears to have been his design. One account records that 'Mr Thomas Sandby was busily engaged in placing the numerous stones to form the representation of rocks and caverns at the head of Virginia Water and frequently dug for stones at Bagshot Heath. Fortunately, he discovered one of an enormous size, which he thought would afford him a massive breadth in his composition, but it was so large he was under the necessity of breaking it with gunpowder. However, fortune favoured his design by blowing it into two nearly equal parts, so that he was enabled to join them in their destined spot with great advantage as to general effect'. Courtenay expressed doubts about Sandby's designs, but Robinson had reservations about interfering. 'I would not meddle with the Rock Work at present', he replied to Courtenay in January 1789, 'because I have a Delicacy in taking down anything that Mr Sandby has done'. Clearly the partnership between Sandby and Robinson was not always an easy one.

The labour force was a large one. The excavation of the lake, the planting of the woodlands, the transport of the huge stones for the construction of the cascades were sufficient for the employment of several hundred men. Even in the winter of 1788-89, when many men had been turned off, 40 labourers were employed in planting alone. There are hints from time to time that all was not well. In April 1788 Courtenay reported trouble with the workmen and Robinson replied, 'I have considered the Behaviour of the Man you shewed me at Virginia Water on Wednesday respecting his endeavours to raise a revolt among the Labourers employed in His Majesty's Works'. He asked Courtenay to refer the question of prosecution to Sandby, but the outcome is not recorded. Threats of industrial action of this kind are not likely to have been frequent. Another problem arose because many of the local labourers had to be released in the summer for harvest work. Some work had to be postponed 'until Harvest Men can be again got'.[5] This was one of the reasons perhaps why soldiers were still sometimes used. There are bills for 'Work done by 23rd Regiment of Foot from 29th June to 23rd Sept 1789'. Charles Cole, who was deputising for Courtenay who was ill, wrote to Robinson on 15 June to report that the troops were encamped and described his plans for putting them to work on the roads and the Cascade. 'I really think', he said, 'it may be well and easily done by the Soldiers by Wheel Barrows'.

The expense too was enormous and — another modern touch — Robinson reported that the Treasury was raising difficulties: 'it cannot be helped; in the present State of Things no new Work must be gone on'.[6] One result was the discharge of men, especially when work was slack in the winter. 'I shall feel much pain', he wrote, 'at discharging the poor men at this time'.[7]

The work falls into two main parts. The first was the excavation of the new extension and the construction of the various dams needed to contain the water or to regulate its flow. The dams are discussed in detail, not only the great Cascade but the smaller ones, especially that at the Wick where the two streams came together to form the Wick Pond before feeding the main Water.

It is clear too that much work was done on the older parts of the lake. The famous High Bridge had been damaged beyond repair in the earlier storms and now a 'New Stone Bridge' was built to take its place. Obviously the necessary work in keeping the lake clear of weeds had been neglected and Robinson complained to Sandby: 'The men employed in cleaning Virginia Water, particularly that part above the Bridge to the Chinese Island, cannot accomplish this without the use of Boats. They have cut the grass at the Sides as far as they can work on account of the depth of the water, but further in and in the middle, where the weeds are very thick, it cannot be cut without Boats. I directed an application to be made to H.R.H.'s Boat Keeper [H.R.H. was the Ranger, Henry, Duke of Cumberland] for their purpose, but he refused and had doubts whether he ought to do it'.[8] The Boat-Keeper was William Lanham and the Keeper of the Chinese Island, Susan Waterhouse, so that although details are not easy to find it looks as if both the Royal fleet and China Island, with its temple, were maintained.

The climax of the reconstruction, however, was the making of the great Cascade. Here the lake was contained and the water ran over the Cascade into the stream — the Bourne — and thus under the 'Great West Road' and out of the Park. A Minute of October 1788 said: 'It is proposed to employ a Number of Horses, Carts and Labourers at this work, during the Winter, in Covering the

Head all over with Mould as His Majesty directed, and in Securing the Back of it, which it is thought will require about 19,000 Cubical Yards of Earth in Turfing the Back Slopes of the Head and in finishing the Cascade etc with Heath Stone, which may require a Thousand Ton of Heath Stone'. Some of the stones not only weighed several tons but had to be brought as much as eight miles. There was great difficulty in finding carriages with axle trees sufficiently strong to convey them, but 'it was found that none bore the strain so well as green alder neatly cut'.

There is much discussion about the landscaping of the Cascade. 'It must be done *slopingly* and not quite home to the Perpendicular Rock Work . . . mixt with Earth and good Soil, for Shrubs to grow in', Robinson told Courtenay.[9] A few weeks later Courtenay expressed satisfaction to Robinson with the progress of the work: 'It looks Inimitably well and hope will please you when you see it' and he spoke of 'the Approbation given by the Gentlemen as they pass, who commonly Stop in their Carriages and Express their Approbation'.[10]

The Cascade 1828. *W.A. Delamotte, jnr.*

The Cascade probably first came into operation in the spring of 1789, for in March Courtenay told Robinson, 'I think it will take 2 Inches more to get well over the Cascade'. The water level had, however, to be lowered from time to time to effect repairs and as far on as April 1797 we find a later foreman, William Tough, reporting to Robinson: 'Virginia Water began to Run over the Cascade yesterday morning and by the middle of the Day made a very fine Cascade'. One thing is clear, namely, that the local residents were still fearful. Even in 1807 the then foreman reported that 'he would be cautious in letting too much water down in wet weather' and spoke of the need 'to quiet the apprehensions of the people of this part of the Country who were very much alarmed at seeing so large a body of water pent up — after being nearly drowned by the breaking of the old head'.[11]

The work was not accomplished without accidents. There are surgeons' bills and correspondence about treatment for accidents to workmen. Peter Smith, for example, had been crippled by a fall of earth. He was an old soldier, with 22 years in HM service, in the 41st and 11th Regiment of Foot and now 'an Out-Pensioner of Chelsea'.[12]

The planting of trees and shrubs was on a colossal scale. One account credits Robinson with planting 'millions of acorns and 20,000 oak trees'. A Nursery was established at the very outset of the work. 'I have begun a Royal Nursery on Wednesday last', wrote Courtenay to Robinson in

September 1788; 'we are Clearing, Stubbing, Scouring, Fencing and draining it, which must be done preparatory to the Trenching and Stocking it etc. I can with much confidence assure you, I think no Situation or Soil in the province more fitt, and when well handled and prepared in its first Procedure, will show the Propriety of this Situation in its future success for the Growth of Timber Trees. I have four men Gathering Weymouth Pine Cones and we must now continue to gather Cones, Berrys and many other Seeds, as they will the sooner Mature this dry season, than otherwise they would be and if not attended, the birds will take the first and best . . . I have collected some of the pods of the Water Lilly, when I was staking, they are now just ripe for sowing in the side of your ponds. I have just hit the right time for them, as they would soon drop off to the bottom of the pond and sow themselves'. Duke William in the 1750s had exploited the resources of the American colonies. In the forty years since then 'the American colonies' had become the United States of America and there is no suggestion of any new attempt to go direct to American sources. However, increasing world trade and travel brought to late eighteenth century Europe a flood of exotic plants, whose period of flowering greatly extended the potential season for gardens of every kind. One new source which Robinson used was a nursery at Perth in Scotland. Here, so he had been informed, 'all kinds of young Forest Trees, Seedlings etc can be had at very small Prices and conveniently and reasonably brought by Shipping to London and by Barges to Old Windsor'.[13]

Lists of trees and shrub seeds wanted for the Nursery were drawn up. Almost every species of British deciduous tree was listed. In addition there was an extensive list of conifers, including four kinds of spruce — Norway, Black and White American and Hemlock — and three each of Cedar and Pine. Many of these still flourish in the Valley Garden and in the woodlands that surround Virginia Water. Among shrubs and smaller trees Rhododendron, Azaleas, Lilacs, Catalpa and Clematis appear in the lists.

Care was needed to protect the young trees against predators. Paling had to be erected to prevent the deer from doing harm. Rabbits were a pest: 'Mr Robinson therefore submits whether His Majesty would not be pleased to give orders totally to extirpate the Rabbits'. Pigs grubbed up many seedlings almost as soon as they had been planted and Robinson wrote angrily to Sandby: 'Hoggs are not fit things for a Park, they are perpetually rooting everything up and you are sensible they must do infinite damage in the grounds planted with Acorns'.[14]

Right in the midst of the work at Virginia Water the King was taken ill. This was the onset of the malady that in later years came increasingly to overshadow his life. The first attack came in the summer of 1788 and in November he was, against his wishes, removed from Windsor to Kew, where his physicians considered he could enjoy greater privacy and be able to take exercise in the garden. Those in charge of the work at Virginia Water heard the news of his illness with anxiety. At the beginning of March in the following year Courtenay referred to 'the relapse of His Majesty's Malady, which God avert for the good of his People'. Several days later Robinson reported, 'Thanks to the Almighty, His Majesty goes on as well as can be wished'. By the 19th he was well enough to return to Windsor, Fanny Burney recording in her **Diary** 'everything and everybody were smiling. All Windsor came out to meet the King'. The King was in fact to enjoy several years of good health before his illness recurred. But the threat remained a shadow over his life and one result seems to have been that the interest he had shown in the making of the new lake never resulted in the enjoyment and pleasure in its use that should have followed. The Royal farms came to occupy a greater place in the King's interests and activities.

Nonetheless, despite setbacks and problems, the present Virginia Water was created in the years 1788-90. There had been preparations in the years before, notably in the acquisition of the land required. The work continued in the years following. The creation of the extended and reconstructed lake in its framework of woodlands belongs, however, to this short period of two or three years.

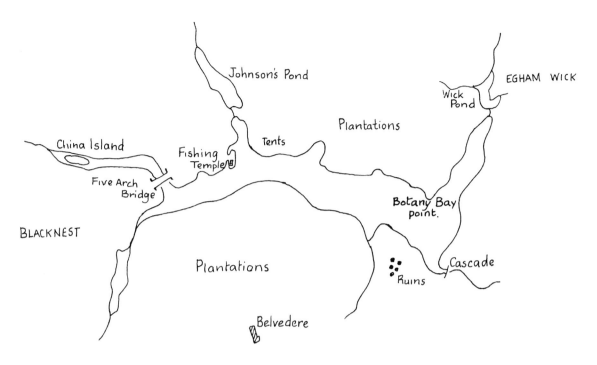

The Second Lake, showing the extension in the time of George III c1790, and some of George IV's developments in the 1820s.

George IV driving by Sandpit Gate in the Great Park. *From R. Huish, Memoirs of George IV 1830.*

'A Kingfisher'. The cartoon that angered George IV, 1826.

George IV's Chinese Temple (from the rear). (RL)

Prinny's Gilded Toy

The onset of George III's malady became more persistent after 1800. The final illness began in 1810 and for another ten years he lingered on, a pathetic and helpless figure, until death at long last released him. The King's illness is now diagnosed as porphyria, a disease caused by an imbalance in the pigments in the cells of the human body which are known as porphyrins. It has many unpleasant symptoms and in acute stages, as with George III, can lead to delirium and delusions. Porphyria was, however, unknown to medical science at the beginning of the nineteenth century. So everyone at the time thought he was mad and his treatment accorded with this diagnosis.

George, Prince of Wales, assumed the Regency in February 1811 when it became clear that there was no hope of another Royal recovery and, when his father died in 1820, he succeeded to the throne as King George IV. He remained King until his own death at Windsor in 1830.

There could hardly have been a greater contrast of characters than that between father and son. Whatever his limitations — and they were many — George III was often kindly and aimiable in his private life. George IV, though he knew how to charm and how to entertain, was vain, volatile, extravagant, self-indulgent.

As long as he lived, Windsor Castle remained an asylum for George III and the home of Queen Charlotte and the 'sisterhood' of her five unmarried daughters. The Prince Regent decided therefore to make Cumberland Lodge his Windsor residence. He had hardly, however, made the decision when a fire caused such serious damage that the Lodge had to be extensively re-built. Sir Jeffry Wyatville was the architect and, while the Prince Regent was waiting for the Lodge to be made habitable again, he decided to occupy the Lower Lodge, where Thomas Sandby had lived.

What was originally intended, however, to be a temporary makeshift lasted until 1830. Not that the Prince was satisfied with the Lower Lodge as it was. With the help of John Nash, it was transformed and fitted up in the sumptuous style which accorded with his lavish tastes. The gardens too were superb, with — of course — peacocks on the lawns. 'His rage for alterations was boundless', wrote one of George IV's first biographers, Robert Huish, 'and the only thing which he would not alter, or which he considered did not require altering, was himself'.[1]

The new Lower Lodge — the King's Cottage or the Royal Lodge as it now came to be known — was bizarre. Most things associated with George IV were in fact magnificent or grotesque or both. The Royal Pavilion at Brighton, re-built between 1815 and 1822, was his most flamboyant fantasy, and he continued to use it as one of his principal residences until well on into the 1820s. But Windsor increasingly attracted him. He did not, however, move into the Castle after his father's death. The Castle too had to be transformed. With Jeffry Wyatville again as architect, the reconstruction of the Castle began in 1824. George IV was able to make use of the Castle at the very end of his reign and it was here that he died, but the creation of what was in effect a *new* Royal palace of romantic grandeur was not complete until 1836. It was in the luxurious Royal Lodge in the Park that he found the seclusion which enabled him to put the world of public affairs out of sight and, when he wished, out of mind. William Cobbett, that most determined of radicals, once tried to petition the King here. He did not get further than 400 yards from the Lodge. Sir Owen

Morshead relates in his book, *George IV and Royal Lodge*, how the King had his own private way from the Castle to the Park and 'had rides so arranged . . . that he had between 20 and 30 miles of neatly-planted avenues from which the public were wholly excluded. At certain points of these rides which open towards the public thoroughfares of the park there were always servants stationed on these occasions, to prevent the intrusion of strangers upon the King's privacy'. Cobbett himself, passing through the Park in 1822 on one of his 'rural rides', commented: 'A very large part of the park is covered with heath or rushes, sure sign of execrable soil. But the roads are such as might have been made by Solomon'.[2]

There were extensions and improvements in every part of the Park. The Belvedere, the little triangular 'fort' on Shrubs Hill, was enlarged by Wyatville, who added turrets and additional rooms including an octagonal dining room. On the terrace the Duke of Cumberland's cannon were deployed to make provision for the firing of salutes on suitable occasions. There was a menagerie at Sandpit Gate, with wapities and chamois and gazelles. Later, there was the huge equestrian statue of George III on Snow Hill at the southern end of the Long Walk. George IV did not live to see the erection of the statue, which took place in 1831, but he laid the foundation stone in August 1829. One would like to think that the inscription 'GEORGIO TERTIO, PATRI OPTIMO, GEORGIUS REX' was inspired by a contrite heart and a stricken conscience.

George IV was passionately fond of angling. He was accustomed to fish in the Thames from the Home Park until in 1826 a scurrilous cartoon carrying the title 'A King-Fisher', and showing the King with his friend Lady Conyngham, angered him so much that he turned to Virginia Water. The lake provided him with the privacy he desired for his recreation. But 'the simple pleasures of life' had no meaning for him. Everything he did was ostentatious and Virginia Water became his 'gilded toy'. He built a new Chinese Fishing Temple, bigger and more ornate than its eighteenth century predecessor on the Chinese Island. The vitriolic Robert Huish, describing the Temple, commented that for its building and decoration 'thousands were extracted from the public purse to enable royalty and the paramour of royalty to angle for minnows and sticklebacks'.[3]

The lake had been neglected during the illness of George III, so that in any case a great deal of work needed to be done. At the eastern end there were major repairs to the Cascade. The water had penetrated and washed away much of the earth, so that there was a danger of collapse. A new grating was placed above the Cascade 'to prevent Fish going out of the Pond'. At the other end China Island was tidied up and the lake deepened and cleared of weeds.[4] Five Arch Bridge, the stone bridge which had replaced the original wooden 'High Bridge' in 1790, was re-built in 1826 to create a bridge architecturally imposing and still able today to cope with the demands of modern traffic.

The new Chinese Temple, with three octagonal spires and dragon-crowned turrets, was the most colourful of George IV's new follies at Virginia Water. This was on a small island on the northern shore of the lake, where the ancient manor lodge had been situated. One or more bridges connected it to the 'mainland'. It was in fact a new China Island, although that name continued to be borne by the original eighteenth century island at the western end of the lake. The Temple is again attributed to Wyatville, although it is probably based on designs by an architect named Frederick Crace, who had earlier done work for the Royal Pavilion at Brighton. The Temple was set at the edge of the lake and a long gallery over the water extended the whole length of the building. The exterior was brilliantly coloured. Charles Greville, the diarist, who visited it soon after the King's death, described it as 'beautifully ornamented, with one large room and a dressing room on either side, a kitchen, offices etc, and in a garden full of flowers, shut out from everything'.[5] A larger building, also in 'the Chinese taste', appears in the background in illustrations and Robert Huish, writing in 1830, probably had both buildings in mind when he commented on 'the inharmonious introduction of these fantastical buildings, amidst the natural luxuriance of the spot'.[6] Other accounts mention an aviary and a fountain stocked with golden and silver carp.

44

To the east of the Fishing Temple island was the wide creek which leads from Johnson's Pond to the main lake. On the slopes above the opposite bank were a number of tents. Greville described them as 'communicating together in separate compartments and forming a very good house, a dining room, drawing room, and several other small rooms, very well furnished'.[7] In the summer the King used to dine every day either in the Temple or in the tents. These dinner parties often continued for three or four hours or more, for the King was capable of consuming gargantuan meals and could get through two or three bottles of claret before rising from the table.

The daily outings to Virginia Water were described by a number of those who took part in them. Lady Shelley, a member of the King's entourage, recorded in her diary: 'They meet at three o'clock, at which hour five or six phaetons come to the door, each to receive a lady and gentleman who drive about the country until five. At that hour the whole party dine on the shore of Virginia Water . . . The party sit at table until between 9 and 10 o'clock, then they return to the Cottage, dress *presto*, and go into the saloon where they play at écarté and other games until midnight. It is every day the same. Oh! monotony!'

Another unwilling participant was the Duke of Wellington, who echoed Lady Shelley's sentiments about what he called this perpetual 'junketing' which lasted 'from morning till night'. He wrote to his friend, Mrs Arbuthnot, one summer day in 1824: 'We embarked yesterday at three, and were upon the lake of Como, either in the boat or dining, till nine. We then returned, dressed as quickly as possible and passed the night at Ecarté and supper from which we broke up about one, thus passing ten hours in company! In my life I never heard so much nonsense or folly or so many lies in the same space of time . . . We are to have a repetition of the same today, as I see that unfortunately it is a fine day'.

The Chinese Temple from the Lake, with boats and tents. *From R. Huish,*
Memoirs of George IV, 1830.

The Duke of Cumberland had put his hand deeply into his own pocket to find the money for the works carried out in the Park in the mid-eighteenth century. There are no indications that George IV ever demeaned himself by emulating his great-uncle's example. There is a pertinent comment, for instance, that relates to the tents. Thomas Creevy, as Treasurer of the Ordnance, wrote to a friend on 30 June 1831: 'I have been given a curious receipt upon a curious subject. The Duke of Wellington and Sir William Knighton have this day paid me £3,170 as executors of his late Majesty. The money is for tents erected upon that part of Windsor Park called Virginia Water. The canvas comprising the tents is from Ordnance Stores, and as His Majesty was pleased to imagine that whenever he *took the field* his Ordnance Department must supply him with tents, he never meant to pay for these articles . . . What think you of the payment of the artificers who put up these tents — four large and four small ones — being upwards of £2000 out of the £3,170? If such a sum can have been spent upon a few tents what think you of the whole expenditure of the Virginia Water Cottage etc, etc?'[8]

A small fleet of boats was gradually assembled on the lake. The *Windsor Express* for 18 March 1828 reported that 'Captain Charles Inglis's beautiful miniature man-of-war, *"The Victorine"*, the gem of all aquatic picturesque amusements, is to be brought from the Thames at Greenwich, to Virginia Water, for the service of our most gracious Sovereign. Lieut Inglis, son of Captain Inglis, is now at Greenwich arranging for the man-of-war to be brought to Virginia Water. This magnificent craft will prove a valuable and most attractive addition to the Virginia Water Fleet of His Majesty'.

Already there was a 'superb yacht' and a 'royal barge'. The latter seems to have been on the lake since 1823. Illustrations show it with a canopied compartment in the poop for the King and those with him, the 'silken flag of royalty' at the stern, and as many as twenty oarsmen, seated in pairs with their long oars swinging in unison as the vessel traversed the lake. Clearly, there was also a smaller barge (this appears in the illustration of the Duchess of Kent's birthday celebrations in 1842), which was used for the band. This boat was often moored at the lakeside and, when the King went aboard the Royal Barge, he was greeted with the strains of *God Save the King*. It is easy to imagine the Royal pleasure in being rowed on summer evenings on the placid water of the lake in its setting of woodland and gentle hills.

The 'Ruins' by the lakeside also date from the time of George IV.[9] There are two lines of columns facing each other and at right angles to the lake. Some are surmounted by broken entablatures, while scattered around are parts of columns and shafts. Almost all of these are of granite. The more impressive section of the 'Ruins' lies in the grounds of Fort Belvedere, beyond the rather incongruous brick road bridge (this was built in George IV's time to provide him with a carriage drive beneath the existing road). The columns here are of capallino, a white-and-green marble. They are again broken and in some cases only the base and a fragmented section of the shaft remain, but they are formed into a semi-circular apse which has some claim to be called picturesque. In the spring, clumps of primroses add a touch of colour to the rather sombre setting. There were originally also statues and inscribed stones, but most or all of these have disappeared over the years.

The presence of the 'Ruins' here is entirely in accord with George IV's other follies at Virginia Water. They came from the Roman-built port and city of Lepcis Magna, some seventy miles to the east of the city of Tripoli on the Mediterranean coast of North Africa. In the second and third centuries AD Lepcis was a place of considerable size. It declined with the decline of the Roman Empire itself and much of it disappeared beneath the sand. The very sand, however, which overwhelmed it helped to preserve it from neglect.

In 1816 the English Consul-General at Tripoli, Col Hanmer Warrington, persuaded the Bey to offer to the Prince Regent some of the columns and other architectural remains at Lepcis. The Bey clearly regarded this as an inexpensive way of promoting a friendship with his fellow Bey in England and was delighted to agree. Warrington himself had been a crony of the Prince Regent. He was a colourful character, a great drinker, a hard swearer and an inveterate gambler — it was said that he once lost £40,000 to the Prince in a single night's play. He was accompanied to Lepcis by Rear-Admiral W.H. Smyth, who was an antiquarian as well as a naval officer of high rank. Like some of his contemporaries he saw nothing wrong in removing classical antiquities and transporting them to England. For him Lepcis was a magnificent spoil-heap which would yield an inexhaustible supply of columns, sculptures and entablatures.

The chief problem arose from the sheer bulk and weight of the stones and it was some little while before arrangements could be made for the necessary transport. In the meantime the local inhabitants, alerted to the impending loss of their supply of building materials, removed parts of the columns. In particular they cut away the necking and base mouldings of some of the columns to provide millstones to grind olives.

Eventually, in October 1817, the storeship *Weymouth* arrived and such columns and other fragments as could be fitted into the hold of the ship were loaded. Smyth reported: 'I had the satisfaction to perceive the mighty masses embarked and stowed away at the rate of at least 60 tons a day'. Three marble columns proved to be too large and had to be left lying on the beach. The *Weymouth* reached Malta on 19 November, but there were then further delays and England was not reached until March 1818. At some point what was intended as a personal gift to the Prince Regent was now to be accepted as a present to the British Government. However, neither the Foreign Office nor the Admiralty showed much interest; nor for that matter did the Prince Regent himself at this stage. So the columns ended up in the courtyard of the British Museum, where they remained for some six years.

The next chapter of the story began in August 1824 when a letter from Sir Charles Long, friend of the Prince Regent (now George IV) and also a Trustee of the British Museum, communicated 'His Majesty's commands that the Columns and Fragments deposited in the Courtyard of the Museum should be placed at the disposal of his architect, Mr Jeffry Wyatt, to whom His Majesty had given further instructions concerning them'.

The 'Ruins', with Virginia Water in the background 1828.
W.A. Delamotte, jnr.

Another two years of obscurity followed, but then in its issue of 2 September 1826 the *Windsor Express* reported that on the previous Monday morning at 5 o'clock (this would be 28 August) 'a detachment of the Royal Engineers left Woolwich for the British Museum for the purpose of removing the magnificent remains of the capitals, columns etc which for so long have lain neglected in the Museum Court Yard. The ruins are being taken to Virginia Water and re-erected on a site near the Falls at the express wish of His Majesty. On Monday the Engineers, 40 strong, succeeded in

47

removing three columns, one of which alone weighed eight tons. Twelve horses were needed to haul the huge wagons from the Museum to Virginia Water. It will take more than six weeks to complete the operation'.

The removal and re-erection of the columns was completed by mid-October. There was obviously considerable public interest and much speculation. There were rumours that the ruins formed part of the Elgin marbles, but the *Windsor Express* of 14 October gave reasonably accurate details of their origin. Mock classical ruins were fashionable features of the landscape architecture of this period and what Jeffry Wyatt (now Sir Jeffry Wyatville) did was to use the material to represent a ruined antique temple. The 'Ruins' were in fact graced by the name of *A Temple of Augustus*, but this was merely a 'pretty conceit'. The lay-out was clearly arranged with much care, but it had no relation to any original arrangement at Lepcis Magna.

For additional embellishments a number of statues and other architectural fragments, said to have been captured in a French ship during the wars against Napoleon, were brought from the Wolsey (now the Albert Memorial) Chapel in Windsor Castle, where they had been for some years.

So Virginia Water, with its Chinese Fishing Temple at one end and the Roman Ruins at the other, acquired an aroma of fantasy which expressed the eccentric tastes and the expensive habits of 'the Prince of Pleasure'. As men of the next generation looked back, however, criticism mounted. Charles Knight, the celebrated Windsor journalist, for instance, in his *Journey Book of Berkshire*, published in 1840, commented acidly: 'Real ruins, removed from the sites to which they belong, are the worst species of exotics. The tale which they tell of their old grandeur is quite out of harmony with their modern appropriation. The ruins here are prettily put together; but they are merely picturesque'.[10]

Two books, also published in the 1840s, had much the same sort of thing to say about the Fishing Temple. Edward Jesse, Surveyor of HM Parks and Palaces, wrote in *A Summer's Day at Windsor*: 'It is impossible not to regret that a more appropriate fishing-house than the present temple was not built. It appears more suitable for a Chinese mandarin than for an English king. A *Waltonian* cottage would have been more in character with the place, and would have added to the effect of the scenery'.[11] Finally, in *Windsor Castle and its Environs*, Leith Ritchie summed up his description of the Fishing Temple by concluding: 'There are gay and gaudy colours, and a profusion of brass and gilding, which present themselves in mortal antagonism with the assumed naturalness of the lake'.[12]

The Chinese Fishing Temple has gone. The Royal fleet of boats is no more. Only the 'Ruins' remain to mystify the present-day visitors who come to Virginia Water.

Their Majesties' Pleasure

'What a *changement de scène*, wrote Charles Greville when he visited Windsor after the accession of William IV. 'No longer George the 4th, capricious, luxurious and misanthropic, liking nothing but the society of listeners and flatterers . . . but a plain, vulgar, hospitable gentleman, opening his doors to all the world'.

George IV had died on 26 June 1830. Within a few weeks, Greville was writing in his diary: 'All the late King's private drives through the Park are thrown open, but not to carriages. We went, however, a long string of four carriages, to explore, and got through the whole drive round by Virginia Water, the famous fishing pagoda, and saw all the penetralia of the late King, whose ghost must have been indignant at seeing us scampering all about his most secret recesses'.[1]

Ten days later, Greville's friend, Lady Sefton, 'asked the King to allow her to see Virginia Water in a carriage, which is not allowed, but which His Majesty agreed to. Accordingly we started, and going through the private drives, went up to the door of the tent opposite the fishing house. They thought it was the Queen coming, or at any rate a party from the Castle, for the man on board the little frigate hoisted all the colours, and the boatmen on the other side got ready the royal barge to take us across. We went all over the place on both sides, and were delighted with the luxury and beauty of the whole thing . . . We had scarcely seen everything when Mr Turner, the head keeper, arrived in great haste, having spied us from the opposite side, and was very angry at our carriages having come there, which is a thing forbidden; he did not know our leave, nor could we then satisfy him that we were not to blame'.[2]

For another century Virginia Water remained a Royal pleasure lake. In 1867 the Chinese Fishing Temple was converted into a Swiss Fishing Cottage, but this was not demolished until 1936. The flotilla of boats, with changes and additions, continued to grace the lake. No place was more beloved by members of the Royal family when the Court was at Windsor. They rode on horseback or in carriages round the lake. They visited the Belvedere. They picnicked at the Fishing Temple (even when it was transformed into a Swiss Cottage, it was still often called the Fishing *Temple*). They were rowed on the water, on special occasions there were festivities, with fireworks and illuminations.

William IV, in the few short years that were left to him of life, soon discovered the attractions of Virginia Water. His own birthday and that of Queen Adelaide were both in August — and August was a month when the Court was often at Windsor. In 1831, the year following his accession, the Queen's birthday on the 13th was celebrated at Adelaide Lodge, the new residence in the Home Park and 'at four o'clock the party went in the royal carriages to Virginia Water, where the day's celebrations were continued.' The *Windsor Express* of 27 August 1831 reported that the King and Queen continued 'to take daily excursions in the Great Park and at Virginia Water where they spend a lot of time on the lake. On Monday their Majesties, with the Court, visited Fort Belvedere. Prince George of Cambridge drove the junior members of the party in his pony phaeton. As it was the King's birthday, the guns at the Fort fired a salute on the party's arrival. The King and Queen with their guests subsequently sat down to an elegant collation in the banqueting room'.

The young Princess Victoria, soon to become Queen, was kept aloof by her protective mother, the Duchess of Kent, who did not approve of the two Royal uncles. There were encounters, however. In 1826, when she was seven, the Princess was staying at Cumberland Lodge with her aunt, the Duchess of Gloucester, who took her over to the Royal Lodge. 'When we arrived', she remembered, 'the King took me by the hand saying "Give me your little paw"'. The next day she went for a drive with her mother and they met the King who was going to Virginia Water in his phaeton. 'And he said, "Pop her in", and I was lifted in and placed between him and aunt Gloucester who held me round the waist. (Mamma was much frightened) I was greatly pleased'.[3] The King took her across the lake in his barge and, on another occason, she was taken fishing. But it was not until she herself ascended the throne in 1837 that she in turn came to know the delights of Virginia Water.

Queen Victoria's *Journal* provides many intimate glimpses into the pleasure she found in the Park and the Lake. Here she found relaxation from affairs of state. 'Moroccan affairs look very threatening', but the Park was all 'extremely pretty', 'quite beautiful' . . . The clichés abound, but her simple delight shines through the unaffected phrasing of her descriptions. Occasionally she is more expansive. 'I have never seen the Park in more luxuriant beauty, the splendid trees all in the richest foliage of the freshest green, which in another few weeks "will deepen and darken"'.[4]

The first visit of her reign to Virginia Water was on 12 September 1837. The Queen drove out from Windsor with her mother in a 'small open carriage'. Ladies of the Court followed in other carriages and the gentlemen 'all *rode* with us. We went to the Fishing Temple and there all got out, and the gentlemen all dismounted. I went on the water (the Virginia Water) in the Barge, with Aunt Louise, Mama, Lady Mary Stopford, Miss Lister, Lady Tavistock, Lady Charlotte Copley, Lord Melbourne and Lord Lilford. Some of the other gentlemen rowed; and Lord Palmerston who joined us there also rowed. After being on the water for some time, we landed, and all remained in the Temple for some time; the little frigate fired a salute, and we then came home, as we went, at a ¼ p 6. It was a very pleasant *Partie*'.[5]

One member of the party was Byron's friend, John Hobhouse, and he recorded his own description. He had, he wrote, 'never looked at the scene before, and could fancy himself on the banks of some Swiss or Tyrolean lake. The Queen and her attendants got into the state barge, with the standard of England flying on it, and were rowed to the opposite bank . . . The Royal Party landed at the Pavilion, and the Queen ordered the frigate to be got under way. This pretty miniature man-of-war was manned by a lieutenant and six sailors. When opposite the Pavilion the frigate began to salute, and fired her one-and-twenty guns with great precision. A very pretty effect was produced by the smoke, burnished by the setting sun, rolling away on the surface of the lake'.

These outings rang the changes on the many possibilities the Park afforded. 'We took a beautiful and very long ride, all round by the opposite side of Virginia Water'.[6] 'It was a beautiful long ride; we rode to the Belvedere on the opposite side of Virginia Water'.[7] 'We rode round Virginia Water, the contrary way to the other day'.[8] 'We rode through the Wood and Plantations *near* Virginia Water, through the Norfolk Farm'.[10] 'We drove through the Rhododendron Drive, by the Obelisk, and round the inner side of Virginia Water'.[11] Some of the Queen's entries give the impression that she could hardly wait for the opportunity to visit the lake. For example, she returned to Windsor from Buckingham Palace on 17 August 1839. It was a wet day, but 'at 5 it ceased raining. We set off in the pony carriages for Virginia Water . . . When we got to the Fishing Temple we had refreshments there, after which we went on the water in the Barge'.[12] She took great pleasure in showing Virginia Water to her visitors and was delighted with their appreciative comments. Louis Philippe, King of the French, came to Windsor on a state visit in October 1844. He was made a Knight of the Garter and afterwards accompanied the Queen into the Park. 'We drove round Virginia Water', she recorded, 'the King after saying : "*il n'y a rien de plus beau que Windsor*"'.[13]

In the early years of her reign the Queen often rode on horseback herself, cantering through the woodland glades with her gentlemen and her ladies. Lord Melbourne, her Prime Minister, was her constant companion and she basked in his avuncular pleasantries. Lord Palmerston, animated and garrulous, also often accompanied the Queen, but never so much in her affections as 'dear Lord Melbourne'. Once, as they were returning from Virginia Water, her horse swerved and threw her. 'I fell on one side sitting', she wrote, 'not a bit hurt, or put out, or frightened, but astonished and amused, — and was up, and laughing, before Col. Cavendish and one of the gentlemen, all greatly alarmed, could come near me and said, "I'm not hurt" . . .'. She records Melbourne's concern, but continues, 'I instantly remounted and cantered home'. The great charm of Queen Victoria's *Journal* is that she was always herself. She records the accident as if it were of no account, but the very next day admits to herself that she was 'rather stiff, all down my right hip, which is somewhat bruised by my fall'.[14] She was riding in the neighbourhood of Virginia Water on four days out of five in the following week.

A change came after her marriage with Albert in 1840. She delighted in introducing Albert to the Park, but it was not long before he (literally) took over the driving seat. 'Albert drove me out' is the refrain of many entries from this time on. They still went to the Fishing Temple and to the Belvedere, but they also went to see Albert's Kennels and Pheasantry at Virginia Water. Albert sometimes went shooting and joined the Queen later. Pheasants were the most usual target, but the deer were also coursed in the Park, as they had been by princes and courtiers over the centuries. On 10 February 1851 the Queen recorded: 'Albert shot 4 roes — such pretty creatures, but they do a deal of mischief'.[15]

Birthday celebrations at Virginia Water, August 1842. *From Queen Victoria's Journal, with a note in her own handwriting: 'Eveng of Aug 17 — Very like'.* (RL)

Soon the children enter the scene. First was the Princess Royal, christened Victoria after her mother and known in the family as 'Vicky'. On 18 August 1841 the Queen wrote: 'Near Virginia Water we met our good little Pussy driving and we took her and Mrs Roberts into our carriage, taking them home'.[16] Next came Prince Albert-Edward ('Bertie'), who was to be the Prince of Wales for

51

almost sixty years before he ascended the throne as King Edward VII. Other princes and princesses followed. They all came to know Virginia Water; some became fond of it. The girls accompanied their mother to the lake and went on the water, while the older boys went shooting with their father.

Virginia Water plays a prominent part in Royal birthday celebrations. Two, in 1842 and 1843, are described by the Queen in some detail and obviously with considerable satisfaction. The first of these was on 17 August 1842, the birthday of the Duchess of Kent. After breakfast with Mama at Frogmore, the Queen was occupied with a report from the Home Secretary, Sir James Graham, about the rioting at Preston, Blackburn and Bolton where there had been a wave of strikes against the reduction of wages. Victoria recorded the report rather summarily and not unnaturally expressed the official view: 'the troops, in self-defence, were compelled to fire, several persons being killed and wounded among the rioters'. When the Queen came to write up her *Journal* on the following day, the industrial troubles had receded and the events of the evening were uppermost in her mind. 'At ½ p 6' she wrote, 'we drove with Papa, Dss [the Duchess of Norfolk], Lehzen and the two Maids of Honour following, to Virginia Water, where at the Fishing Temple, *all* our usual dinner party were assembled . . . A Band was stationed in a boat close, opposite the Temple. We went on the water in the Barge . . . When we returned we found Mama had arrived. We dined in the Fishing Temple at ½ p 7. Mama's health was drunk. By the time dinner was over it had become quite dark and the moon was shining brightly, casting such a lovely reflection in the water. We went down and sat under the upper room, and it was *so* warm and fine. Just as we came down, the smallest Frigate was towed round, all lit up, which had a very pretty effect, — the Band playing *Rule Britannia* and the guns of the Belvedere saluting . . . It was really quite fairy like, looking at the Temple, all lighted up, and going round the illuminated Frigate. We all came home at ½ p 10 driving in open carriages, and it was very pleasant, but it was rather foggy'.[17]

A sketch of the scene appeared in the *Illustrated London News*. The Queen cut it out and added a note in her own handwriting: 'Eveng of Aug 17 — *Very Like*'.

Albert's own birthday also fell in August and in the following year even grander celebrations were staged at the lake. The Queen was ecstatic. 'At 7 we drove to the Fishing Temple at Virginia Water where we were to dine. The room was illuminated as well as the Barge, in which was stationed the Band of the 1st Life Guards. The Band of the Coldstreams was stationed in the garden. Towards the end of dinner my dearest Albert's health was drunk, the Battery and the Belvedere saluting. Afterwards we all went to the verandah and the illuminations and fireworks began. I must say they were extremely pretty and Albert, who is fond of that sort of thing, was very pleased. The Bands were playing the whole time. The Frigate was lit up with coloured lamps, as also two little ships, and they came round opposite to the Fishing Temple. Blue and red lights, and endless rockets were let off, which had such a charming effect reflected in the water. Everything succeeded so well, the evening was so calm and the "*locale*" so beautiful, that nothing could have been nicer and more beautiful. What with the music and the illuminations on the banks and on the water, the effect was quite fairy like. We came home at ½ p 10. My dearest Albert was full of love and tenderness, saying how pleased he was with the whole day, which certainly had been a very happy one. May we see many returns of it, — and my beloved husband be spared to me till a good old age'.[18]

Ten years later, on 5 July 1853, the lake was the scene of a different spectacle in the shape of military manoeuvres. The Royal party travelled to Windsor from London. 'At the Gr. Western station we got into carriages and drove to Virginia Water, where Ld Hardinge [the Commander-in-Chief] met us and with us, got into a large Barge rowed by 6 men of the "Victoria and Albert". The manoeuvres of which I can give no very clear or technical description had begun by a demonstration, tremendous firing from Artillery and Infantry, the smoke of which rose in thick clouds from the roads surrounding Virginia Water. We were rowed up under the bridge and back, the banks being full of soldiers under the trees, who kept up a tremendous cross-fire, which had a very picturesque effect. We then were rowed to the other end, opposite to Turner's [the Keeper's]

Azaleas and bluebells bordering a woodland path
in the Valley Garden. (BT)

The Plunket Pavilion in the Valley Garden. (BT)

house, and here we saw the Sappers and Miners throw a pontoon bridge over Virginia Water. It took about 40 minutes to do, and a pretty sight it was'. The day ended with a march past on Smith's Lawn.[19]

The Queen's visits to Virginia Water were mostly in the summer, sometimes too in the spring or the autumn if the court was at Windsor. In the winter months she was more often at Buckingham Palace and it was not until January 1861 that she records going to Virginia Water on an 'exceedingly cold' winter's afternoon. The lake was 'splendidly frozen over. A good many people there. We were driven on the ice, which was as smooth as glass and afterwards watched a very animated game of Hockey'. On the following morning the Queen went to Virginia Water again and the Royal party were driven in sledges on the ice. Albert and the Princes had gone shooting but in the afternoon they too went to Virginia Water and enjoyed themselves skating.[20]

Before the year was out Albert was dead. Over the forty years that still remained of her reign the Queen never recovered from the shock and the tragedy of her personal bereavement. The light had gone out of her life. It would not be true to say that she gave up going to Virginia Water. But she could no longer take the same pleasure in her visits, as she had done during the many happy excursions with Albert. As the years passed, she went for longer drives in the neighbourhood — Englefield Green, New Lodge, Sunninghill, Datchet. But for some time her horizons when she was at Windsor seemed hardly to extend beyond Frogmore and the Mausoleum where her dear Albert had been laid to rest. She spent less time at Windsor and more at Osborne and Balmoral.

This did not mean she no longer took an interest in Virginia Water. Decisions were often referred to her and reports made to her, even when she was at far away Balmoral. She was asked for her approval for the Prince of Wales to have a sailing boat on the lake and gave it, providing it was safe. Complaints about the insanitary condition of the lake were reported to her. She was consulted about requests for the use of the lake. She was told about the dangerous condition of the 'Ruins', and replied: 'These stones may be pulled down as suggested and allowed to remain where they fall'.[21]

The Royal Family could come and go; their interest in the lake could rise and fall. Some measure of continuity was provided by Captain David Welch of the Royal Navy. He was appointed to the office of 'Keeper of Her Majesty's Boats and other Vessels at Virginia Water' in September 1861 at a salary of £150 per annum.[22] He was still in the position at the time of his death in 1912, over fifty years later. He was then over 90 years of age and had progressed to the title of Sir David Welch KCVO. At first he was based on Portsmouth, but later he came to live in the newly-built Virginia Water Cottage, the house built on the slope above the Fishing Temple. He was appointed as Keeper of Virginia Water Fishing Temple and Cottage in 1890. There are hints that he did not move with the times. One of the first actions of his successor, Captain George Broad, was to ask for a telephone and an efficient drainage system at the Cottage. There was some discussion about the use of trees as against poles for the telegraph wires, but the King (George V) insisted that the Post Office must put everything underground.[23]

Welch was obviously very much liked by members of the Royal Family. The future George V, who was often at Virginia Water, especially in Ascot Week, refers to this spry retired naval officer as 'little Welch' and makes the comment that he was 'in good form' — which probably meant that he had a fund of good stories.[24] The scores of letters which he wrote to the various officers of the Royal Household and others testify to the assiduous and conscientious way in which he discharged his duties. He was constantly badgering his superiors about the condition of the boats, of the boathouses, of the lake itself.

The most revealing instance of Welch's concern about the condition of the lake was in 1885. There was a flurry of letter-writing when Welch reported that Virginia Water was dangerously insanitary. 'For years', he wrote, 'the rushes and weeds have been allowed undisturbed . . . in the different creeks (notably China Island, Blacknest and Egham Wick). Where twenty years since a boat can be taken, they are now unapproachable, the result of which is that in a dry summer like the present . . . the stench is unsupportable, more especially at Blacknest'. Asiatic cholera was raging on the Continent and, if Virginia Water was allowed to be a 'fever and cholera Den', the danger could be a real one. There was some scepticism about Welch's report, but the medical journal, the *Lancet*, was taking an interest and there was a fear that the name of a member of the Royal Family such as Prince Christian, the current Ranger, might be brought in. It was easy to diagnose the problem. 'As you must be aware', wrote one Royal official, 'it is extremely difficult to know how to deal with a large area of water comparatively stagnant as is the case with Virginia Water and into which masses of foliage are constantly falling and the weeds grow with an extraordinary rapidity, all of which tends to block up the water way'. But there was general agreement that something must be done and the lake was dredged.[25]

In 1867, as we have seen, George IV's Chinese Fishing Temple was transformed into a Swiss Cottage. Fashions had changed and the passion for *chinoiserie* which had produced not only the Temple at Virginia Water but the grandoise Pavilion at Brighton had diminished. The Chinese Temple had lasted for forty years; the Swiss Cottage was to grace the lakeside scene for another seventy. It still preserved some of the features of the earlier building such as the interior rooms and the balcony above the lake.

The Office of Woods and Forests, the government department which had charge of the Royal estates, was responsible for the maintenance of the Fishing Cottage. George IV, however, had succeeded in the 1820s in getting the Admiralty to provide for the frigate, the barge and the yacht that formed the nucleus of the Royal flotilla. In William IV's reign a new frigate named in honour of his Queen, the *Royal Adelaide*, was added. The chequered history of the little fleet is not easy to follow, all the more because the use of many nautical terms such as frigate, brig, galley, gig, wherry, skiff and barge does not always make for clarity. From time to time the Admiralty tried ineffectually to rid itself of the responsibility for this superfluous addition to the country's naval forces. The *Royal Adelaide* was in such a bad state of repair by 1862 that the question of a completely new frigate was raised. W.G. Romaine of the Admiralty wrote to Sir Charles Gore of the Office of Woods and Forests: 'I should think a new frigate would cost two or three thousand pounds complete, and of course there is no sum tabled in this year's estimates. Is this vessel ever used or is it only retained as an ornament to the lake?' The Queen herself expressed the opinion that 'she wanted the vessel to be "ornamental" only'. So repairs were decided on. Welch, who had raised the matter in the first instance, became more and more exasperated by the delays. He asked for an early decision *'if it is possible for the Woods and Forests to decide anything'*. When he was given approval to go ahead, he then said it was too late in the year to do the work. In the next spring the Admiralty was still prevaricating about putting the cost of the 'ornamental' boats at Virginia Water on the Navy Estimates.[26] The controversy surfaced from time to time over the years, but when the little fleet was finally dispersed in 1936 the officer in charge reported that 'the whole job . . . was carried out at the Admiralty's expense'.[27] In 1873 the War Office 'made provision for 'the supply of the ammunition demanded for the use of the *"Royal Adelaide"* Frigate at Virginia Water', presumably for the firing of salutes.[28] In 1877, however, an Admiralty survey showed that its timbers were rotten and recommended that it be broken up. This recommendation was carried out in the autumn of the same year.[29]

In the meantime the condition of the Royal Barge was giving cause for concern. In the summer of 1873 Welch reported that 'this boat has been in constant use the last ten years for the Royal personages who have visited Virginia Water, but in consequence of the bad state she is now in, it was found impossible to use her on the visit of H.M. the Shah of Persia to this place last week. As we have now no boat fit for the reception of Royalty I have to request that you will be pleased to move the Lords Commissioners of the Admiralty either to put this boat in a state of repair or to supply us with a new one'.[30] The Admiralty unexpectedly decided to provide a completely new Royal Barge 'at a very great cost . . . for the use of Her Majesty at Virginia Water'.[31] Welch wanted the new Barge in time for the visit of the Emperor of Russia, Alexander II, in May of the following year and, when the Admiralty expressed doubts if the new vessel could be ready in time, made the impatient comment: 'It is not every day we get a live Emperor in this part of the world'.[32] Arrangements were, however, made for 'the small Admiralty Barge now at South Kensington being conveyed to Virginia Water for the use of Her Majesty at the commencement of May'.[33] It was just as well that this arrangement was made, as the new State Barge was not ready for delivery until December 1875.[34]

Welch took great pride in the new Barge. 'She is beautifully turned out' was his comment on one occasion. His chief worry now seemed to be the condition of the Boathouse in which the Barge was kept. 'I cannot keep the Barge on the water', he wrote in 1903, 'or she will be water sodden. What I am to do with her I know not, at any rate I cannot take responsibility of this boat being ruined after the Admiralty spending such a large sum of money on her'.[35] Two years before, in April 1901, the Barge had been fitted up with electricity at a cost of £150.[36] The Queen had died in January and presumably this action was taken on the initiative of the new King Edward VII. He had in fact originally wanted a new electric launch, but had to be content with something less.

Other boats made their appearance on Virginia Water from time to time. Two early boats are mentioned by Welch: 'The Galley is a four-oared boat built for the Duchess of Kent in 1841. The White Boat [this is probably the one referred to by George V as the *White Rose*] was built in 1840, the other two boats in 1850, the skiff was here when I came in 1861, but I don't know when she was built'.[37] In 1876 'a sort of Indian Launch' arrived from Calcutta for the Prince of Wales.[38] In 1904 a Royal Brig *King Edward VII*, originally a 42-feet Launch, was converted and rigged out to scale as a ten gun brig. She was fitted out at Sheerness Dockyard and towed up the Thames to Brentford, whence she was taken by road to Virginia Water. In 1919, on being surveyed, the hull was found to be 'in a very bad condition of dry rot which would run into great expense to make good'.[39] The Admiralty accordingly ordered that she should be broken up. Among the boats still at the lake in 1936 was a Canadian birch bark canoe, which had been presented in 1901 to the future George V and Queen Mary by the lumbermen of Ottawa Valley.

Use of the lake was always controlled, and was generally restricted to members of the Royal Household. Requests from local country gentlemen to have a boat on the Water were normally refused. Sandhurst Cadets were allowed to use Virginia Water for rowing practice in 1919, but the authorities were not happy about what they regarded as a departure from tradition.[40]

What really set the cat among the pigeons was the use of Virginia Water in 1931 for speed-boats by the Prince of Wales (the future King Edward VIII and Duke of Windsor). His brother, the Duke of Kent, and several of the Prince's friends joined him. Some of the boats arrived at the lake without prior warning. The authorities were extremely worried about the dangers. The Keeper reported: 'A life buoy is in readiness on the landing stage. I have satisfied myself that my personel are familiar with the latest method of re-suscitating the apparently drowned'. This was followed by a note in red typescript: 'A speed boat capsized the other day. The occupant had no belt on and was recovered by the row-boat as he was clinging to the fin keel. It would be dangerous to wade ashore in most places on account of the depth of vegetable ooze'.[41]

Five years later it was the same Royal personage, now King Edward VIII, who ordered the demolition of the Fishing Cottage and the dispersal of the boats. By this time the Cottage was in a decrepit state and its demolition was strongly urged by the Crown Estate Commissioners on the grounds of its almost total decay.[42]

In September E.H. Savill, the Deputy Ranger, recorded: 'the Royal Barge is going to Portsmouth, the Sailing Cutter to Dartmouth, the Canadian Canoe to Chatham and the small Royal Barge and the 12 foot dinghy *Prince George* to the Training Ships 'Arethusa' and *Mercury*'.[43]

For many years the use of Virginia Water by members of the Royal Family had been declining and the events of 1936 marked the end of an era. Henceforward Virginia Water would be what it is today, one of the finest lakes in England, no longer the preserve of Royalty but open to all who come to enjoy its beauty.

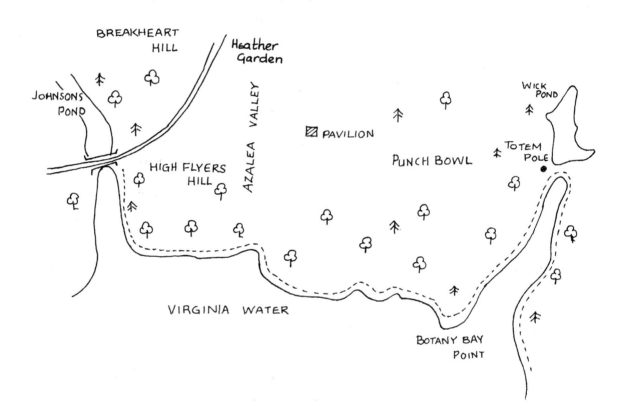

The Valley Garden, showing a few of the main features at the present day.

The Valley Garden

On the northern shore of Virginia Water is the Valley Garden, lying between the lake itself and Smith's Lawn.

The Valley Garden, as we know it today, has been developed since 1945, but the present Garden has a continuity with the original landscaping of the eighteenth century. It was then that the slopes and undulations above the lake were fashioned, to provide the combination of art and nature in which the landscape architects delighted. Valleys, bordered with flowering shrubs and tall trees, lead the eye upwards to the ridge that frames the view. Looking back, there are glimpses of the lake itself and the woodland beyond. No two parts of the Garden are alike, for 'unity in diversity' is the prevailing feature.

Some of the trees go back to the original eighteenth century plantings. Where in Sandby's drawings there are views over open country there are now conifer plantations and deciduous woodland, with almost every variety of English tree and many trees of foreign origin also. Some trees have reached and passed maturity in recent years and have had to be felled and replaced. Thus the majestic stand of beeches, on rising ground half-way along the shore, dominating the lake and providing a magnificent feast of colour in the autumn, had to go — although some trees remain on the bank above the lake itself.

The western extremity of the Valley Garden borders the park road from Blacknest to Smith's Lawn. This passes over two arms of Virginia Water, the first by way of Five Arch Bridge, the second by Johnson's Pond. It then ascends Breakheart Hill (this intriguing name occurs at least as early as 1789). To the left is a plantation of flowering cherries, with colourful blossom in the spring and resplendent foliage in the autumn. To the right the slopes of the Garden rise steeply. As almost everywhere in the Garden, rhododendrons are the dominant shrub. Much of the original Rhododendron species collection was moved to the Garden from Tower Court, Ascot, after the death of J.B. Stevenson in 1951. He had spent fifty years amassing the collection and many new species have been added to it since. Some are North American species; others have their origin in China, Japan or Nepal. Many are already in flower in April, but the height of the flowering season comes in June. One especially beautiful shrub is *Rhododendron calophytum* from Swechwan, which has white flowers with deep red markings inside. When the rhododendrons have finished flowering and the shrubs revert to the deep green of their foliage, the hydrangeas take over. They rise in banks above the road with their flowers of powder-blue and pastel pink. One species has the aristocratic name of *Générale Vicomtesse de Vibraye* and has flowers of a glorious blue to match the splendour of the name.

In the spring there are carpets of narcissi on both sides of the road. Later there are many hundred flowering spikes of Spotted Orchid, their pale pink contrasting with the deeper red of campions.

From the road a path ascends the slopes towards the Heather Garden. Scots Pines rise high above ornamental maples, whose foliage varies in colour from green to rich copper. A Tulip Tree, *Liriodendron tulipifera*, from North America, with its striking spade-shaped leaves, adds variety. There are others on the opposite side of the park road. Groups of Hostas, the Plantain Lily, some tall with dark green leaves, others smaller with light green leaves edged with darker green, make effective ground cover. Most abundant is *Hosta lancifolia*, prominent in June and July, with pale lilac flowers on tall stalks. The Foamflower, *Tiarella cordifolia*, which is in flower right through from April to August, is another attractive plant, with spikes of delicate starry white flowers rising above dense strawberry-shaped leaves. There are glimpses through the trees back to the road below and at one point the prospect opens on to a valley that eventually forms one of the heads of the Azalea Valley. Here are towering conifers, some with the silver foliage which gives them a frosted appearance.

Some way to the east of the park road is High Flyers Hill, crowned with Scots Pines which have the effect of making the hill seem higher than it really is. On one side of the hill is an enclosure, with small conifers, dwarf rhododendrons, cistus and rock roses. On the edge of the valley beyond the hill is a shapely Japanese Poplar, *Populus maximowiczii*, which is in full leaf as early as April. Below the hill the vista extends to the lake; here are new beds of holly and maple, and near the lakeside — and elsewhere — are some fine Pyramidal Hornbeams, *Carpinus betulus 'Pyramidalis'*, with their branches reaching upwards in perfect symmetry.

The whole area between High Flyers Hill and the park road is a mass of colour in season. Apart from the rhododendrons and the hydrangeas, there are magnificent magnolias, at their best in April or even earlier. The *Magnolia sprengeri 'Diva'* from Western China with its pinkish white flowers contrasts with *Leonard Messel* with deep mauve pink. The delicate pale pink flowers of the Japanese Cherry, *Prunus 'Kanzan'*, provide another contrast, this time with the yellow of Forsythia and the red of Pieris 'Forest Flame'. Here again are *Tiarella cordifolia* and several varieties of Hosta. A shrub which is in flower in August is *Eucryphia glutinosa 'Flore-plena'*, with white rose-like flowers. Eucryphia can grow to a considerable height and several tree-like shrubs form a foreground to High Flyers Hill.

One of the glories of the Garden in spring is Azalea Valley. A stream trickles down towards the lake and by its banks are Lysichitums and golden yellow Marsh Marigolds. *Lysichitum americanum* has bright yellow spathes which are followed by large leaves shaped like paddles and often three or four feet long; *L. camschatcense* from N.E. Asia is a smaller plant with white spathes. The marshy swards on either side are bright with daffodils, and clumps of ferns below the birches and the alders make their contribution to the general effect of springtime freshness. Later the flowering of the azaleas which give the valley its name brings about a transformation and, later again, in August the azaleas are followed by hydrangeas, among which *paniculata 'Grandiflora'* with panicles of showy cream flowers is the most striking. On the slopes above and to the right of the valley are two groups of *Salix alba 'Chermesina'*, a White Willow with red-brown stems and leaves silky grey beneath. In a sheltered area near the head of the valley winter days are brightened by the wispy yellow flowers of the Witch Hazel, *Hamamelis mollis*.

Some way further still to the east is a valley which to my mind is the loveliest in the whole of the Garden. It is now dominated by the picturesque Pavilion 'in memory of Patrick Plunket 1923-1975'. Lord Plunket, a friend of the Queen, was Assistant Master of the Royal Household and took great delight in the growth of the Garden. The Pavilion, dedicated on 30 April 1979 by the Queen 'in recognition of his service to the Royal Family 1948-1975', brings a pleasant evocation of eighteenth century landscape architecture. Here again, on either side of the wide green ride that slopes towards the lake, are rhododendrons of many varieties and colours, set among birches, pines and larches. There are beds of hydrangeas too, including again *paniculata 'Grandiflora'*. The smaller trees include flowering Cherries; one particularly beautiful tree is *Prunus serrula* from W. China, which has bands of copper-coloured bark encircling the trunk and branches. Plants of Solomon's Seal border the paths which meander along the sides of the valley and on the lower slopes are stands of Bamboo, Tree Heather, Broom and Maples. *Fothergilla major*, an American shrub from the Allegheny Mountains, has creamy brush-like flowers and there are several varieties of *Thuja orientalis*, an evergreen shrub from China and Japan.

On the banks which rise above the lakeside track are beds of Camellias, which in late April and in May flaunt their white, pale and deep pink flowers. By the lakeside itself, and in some of the valleys also, are Giant Rhubarbs, *Gunnera manicata*, with large rhubarb-shaped leaves four to six or more feet across.

The most spectacular single feature of the Valley Garden is the 'Punch-bowl'. This in mid-May is a feast of exotic beauty when the Kurume Azaleas are in bloom. The Punch-bowl is in the shape of a gigantic amphitheatre, from the higher levels of which there are views downwards towards the lake. The prospect from below is of a semi-circle of massed colour. The display soon passes, but while it lasts it dazzles the eye.

The eastern end of the Garden is more expansive. Paths wander between groves of shrubs and trees, and it is more correct to talk of 'rides' rather than of 'valleys'. There are two of particular interest. One leads towards Botany Bay Point, where there is a break in the thickets of rhododendrons, which both to left and right present an almost impenetrable barrier to the lakeside. Here there is an open area of grass and sand, with views across to the 'Ruins' on the other side of the lake. The ride is bordered by conifers, birches, cherries, maples, rhododendrons — dark red, pink, mauve, cream — and the occasional whitebeam with its glaucous green leaves. By September most of the flowers have finished, but the red berries of Rowan and Viburnum take their place.

Along the top path above the Pavilion is another large plantation of flowering cherries, with pink blossom in spring and, after the lack-lustre of the summer months, glorious in the russet and gold of autumn. Further along the ride there are more magnificent magnolias, conifers, birches, until the incongruous Totem Pole comes into view and, behind, the north-eastern tip of Virginia Water, with Wick Pond to the left of the bridge. At this end the Valley Garden continues to broaden and woodland predominates, extending to the confines of the Park. Much of this is the area 'imparked' at the time of the extension and re-development of the lake at the end of the eighteenth century. The imagination conjures up visions of George III's labourers gathering cones and acorns and seeds and so making possible the creation of these seemingly endless plantations. Here, after two hundred years, is the continuing evidence of their work.

One last feature remains to be mentioned. On the northern edge of the Valley Garden, bordering on Smith's Lawn, is the Heather Garden. It is enclosed and has its own identity. But, unlike the Savill Garden, a mile away beyond Smith's Lawn and the Obelisk Pond, it adjoins the Valley Garden and there are views from it over the Garden and particularly towards Azalea Valley.

The Heather Garden was developed in 1951-1953, with some more recent additions, on the site of an old gravel pit. The beds of heather are colourful at any time of the year, with species in flower in almost every month. The attractiveness of the Garden is, however, now enhanced by a wide range of dwarf and slow-growing conifers. These miniature relatives of what are often majestic forest trees have a fascination all their own. There is, for example, a dwarf Sequoia *sempervirens* '*Adpressa*' of the same family as the giant Redwoods of North America. Its height is only a matter of two or three feet. Its growth is sideways rather than upwards, and the yellow green tips of its foliage give it a delicate beauty difficult to imagine in a larger tree. There are pines, cedars, junipers, cypresses, spruces, yews from many different parts of the world. The tallest are perhaps twenty feet; many are truly dwarf. Their foliage encompasses every shade of green, blending harmoniously with one another. Along with the conifers are cotoneasters with their dark foliage and red berries and berberis with berries of bright orange. Brooms add splashes of golden yellow and sun roses and cinquefoils help to enrich still further the range of colour in the Garden.

The Valley Garden is a cultivated garden, tended constantly, so it is hardly the place where one would expect to see a wealth of wild flowers. The lakeside itself provides more scope, and here, in their season, are Yellow Flag, Yellow Loosestrife, Water Mint, Gipsywort, Meadow Sweet, Water

Dropwort and Water Forget-me-not. On the water itself, in late summer, are water lillies, white, red and yellow, and the pink 'tooth-brush' flower of the Amphibious Bistort. But the grass swards of the Valley Garden are in many places made more colourful by Hawkbits and Hawkweeds, with Tormentil making a foil to the mauve and purple of the heather. It is always a joy too to find Violets, Bird's eye speedwells and Storksbills. There is one wet patch where grow Bog pimpernels, with tiny flowers of palest pink. Mosses and lichens often cover the nakedness of tree stumps and there are areas beneath the trees where a carpet of rich green moss replaces the grass of the more open valleys. The grasses themselves make a contribution to the beauty of the Garden and on many of the banks and slopes they are not cut until August.

For herbaceous borders, rose-beds or formal gardens, the Savill Garden is the place to go and it is here, rather than the Valley Garden, where the visitors come in their thousands to enjoy the feast of colour and beauty. In the Valley Garden can be found quiet and even solitude beneath the canopies of towering trees. Rustic seats invite the walker to rest and, while he sits, he can savour the delights of the flowering shrubs; he can listen to the whistling of the nuthatch, the yaffle of the green woodpecker, the cooing of the wood pigeon, the staccato call of the great tit; or perhaps he will let his eye travel along the vistas that lead to the lake. Sooner or later he will make his way to the lakeside and follow the path that leads to one of the park gates. It is now the lake rather than the Garden that will focus his attention. Framed by trees and shrubs, the water is green rather than grey and the magic of reflection enhances the loveliness of the lake. The water is never still; there is a quiet but continuous motion, caused by the currents of underwater streams, the ripple of the breeze, the trails of ducks and grebes. So the lake and the garden are a unity. Each is essential to the other.

Tufted Duck at Virginia Water.

ABOVE LEFT: Mandarin Drake and Duck at Virginia Water. (GL) RIGHT: Heron. (GL) BELOW LEFT: Canada Goose. (RS) RIGHT: Great Crested Grebe. (GL)

ABOVE: Kurume Azaleas in the Punch Bowl. (RS) LEFT: Beech trees and
the Lake in autumn. (RS) RIGHT: High Flyers Hill in autumn; Maples and
Scots Pines. (RS)

Birds of the Lake

One of the critics of George IV's follies at Virginia Water made the comment: 'It is possible to imagine that the Romans were once here, but NOT the Chinese'. And lo, in the twentieth century, the Chinese have arrived in the form of the Mandarin ducks, which have re-introduced into the Park the exoticism of the Orient. They must be given pride of place here because Virginia Water, along with the rest of the Park and Forest, has become over the last fifty years their most important habitat in Britain. There are certain times of the year and certain times of the day when it is easier than others to find them, but no one who visits Virginia Water regularly can fail to see them. Many writers have gone into raptures over the plumage of the drake, with its brilliant colours and, most striking of all, the magnificent upstanding golden-orange 'fans' or 'sails'. By contrast his lady wears a modest plumage of grey — save for the brownish back. During much of the year no male and female could look more different, and yet in 'eclipse' or moult plumage in late summer the drake loses his finery and closely resembles his partner.

China and Japan are the original homes of the Mandarin duck, where for centuries it had a special place in art and literature. This was partly because of its beauty and partly because it was invested with qualities of affection and fidelity. A Chinese poet more than 2500 years ago wrote:

    'The Mandarin duck was faithful.

    How different from the King!'

It is just as well that George IV did not introduce Mandarin ducks to Virginia Water; the temptation to apply the poet's aphorism would perhaps have been too strong to resist.

There are isolated records of Mandarin in captivity in Britain from the mid-eighteenth century onwards and in 1830 a pair was secured for the London Zoo. It has only been in the present century, however, that the Mandarin has become a popular and attractive addition to waterfowl collections in this country. The chief of these was at the Duke of Bedford's estate at Woburn, but there were a number of others scattered around the countryside, among them one at Foxwarren Park near Cobham in Surrey. It is a common practice to allow the young of pinioned birds to go free and it is likely that at least some of the Virginia Water birds came from this collection at Cobham. As early as 1932 a free-flying colony of Mandarin ducks had come into existence in Windsor Great Park and this colony of *feral* birds, birds that is which, although originally introduced by man, have now established a regular breeding stock, has not only continued to hold its own but has spread to several adjoining districts. In fact the number and range of recordings of full-winged birds increases year by year.

It is, however, with the Mandarin ducks at Virginia Water that we are mainly concerned. At the beginning of the year many of the Mandarin are already paired. Some may be on the open water, but most are likely to be found in the various creeks and inlets or beneath the rhododendrons that fringe the lake. The preference for rhododendrons is something probably carried over from the habits of their ancestors in the Far East. Rhododendrons overhanging the water, backed by mature deciduous woodland with streams and ponds — these are the elements of their favoured environment and, where these do not exist, they are not likely to establish themselves. They can be almost completely hidden by the rhododendrons, especially when they perch on the branches as they frequently do. Mandarin are often first seen in flight. They do not fly high and their silhouette is distinctive. They are a small duck, much smaller than a Mallard and their necks are proportionately shorter. Features like the sail feathers of the drakes are not visible in flight but the birds utter a whistling call when on the wing.

By the beginning of spring the Mandarin start to disappear from the lake and, apart from a few bachelor drakes, for some two months it is uncommon to see them. This is their breeding season. The pairs have dispersed over the surrounding countryside in search of suitable nesting sites. The Mandarin are tree-nesters, choosing cavities or holes. Ancient oaks are ideally suited to their needs and it is in the Forest rather than in the Park where these are to be found. So for most of the breeding season the Mandarin live in seclusion, taken up with the domestic life essential to their survival. The duck lays nine to twelve buffish-white eggs in the unlined nest in the tree, and these are incubated by the duck for 28 to 30 days. Very soon after birth, perhaps even within twenty four hours of hatching, the ducklings drop from the nest to the ground. At this stage they are more gristle than bone and can cope with this hazardous enterprise without harm. The duck calls to them from the ground and, when they join her, she will lead them away to water.

One day in late May the first brood appears on Virginia Water, sometimes both parents, sometimes only the duck, with a flotilla of ducklings, brown and buff and downy. By this time there will almost certainly already be several broods of Mallard on the lake. The ducklings are superficially similar; those of the Mallard are yellowish and brown rather than buff and brown and they soon become larger than their counterparts. New broods arrive almost every day. In 1970 and again in the following year there were as many as twenty broods on Virginia Water by June.

Towards the end of June the drake begins to go into moult and for several weeks the lake becomes less colourful because of his absence. By the end of September, however, he is back in the full glory of his new plumage and the autumn is the best time to watch the Mandarin. The young by this time are fully fledged and, although they have suffered many casualties over the preceding weeks, their numbers help to swell the flocks of Mandarin on the lake. For *flock* they do. Although they still love the shelter of the rhododendrons at the lakeside, they often form 'rafts' on the open water which may comprise anything up to one hundred birds. Numbers of between 150 and 200 have been recorded at Virginia Water on several occasions and, for the Park as a whole, as many as 274 were counted in December 1970 — and this probably by no means represents the true total present. It was estimated in 1952 that the population in Windsor Great Park and neighbourhood was 'not less than 400'. It has had its ups and downs since then; the severe winter of 1962-63 took a heavy toll. In recent years there has, however, been a substantial increase in numbers.

Not only are the Mandarin at their most numerous at Virginia Water in the autumn. They are also at their liveliest. There is a great deal of social display, in which the drake makes the most of his colourful plumage both in impressing rival males and the female with whom he will eventually pair. The 'sail' feathers in particular are raised on the back until they stand upright and almost touch the crest. The head is drawn back, the purple breast expanded and the wing slightly spread. The drakes make passes before the duck, they dip their bills in the water from time to time, they bob and flick their heads, they make a show of indulging in preening. So gradually the pairs are formed or re-formed and the way is clear for the continuing courtship displays, which prepare for the period of nesting and breeding which will begin when the winter days are over.

The Chinese temples and the *Mandarin* yacht have long since gone from the lake; today in their place we have the Mandarin ducks — always a delight to the eye.

Ducks and other wildfowl have probably been coming to Virginia Water since the lake was first formed. Birds appear on a number of the eighteenth and nineteenth century illustrations. An engraving of the Duke of Cumberland's *Mandarin* yacht and the Belvedere in 1753 shows a number of Mute Swans. In some of the illustrations of George IV's time there are Mallard on the water and, in one at least, what might be Canada Geese, with long necks stretched characteristically forward. Duck shooting was a pastime of Royalty and gentry well into the present century. At one time vast numbers of Mallard were reared by hand and taken up in baskets to Manor Hill, where they were released gradually for a day's sport with guns.

Nowadays the interest centres on the ducks themselves as they come and go with the seasons. Through the summer the ducks at Virginia Water are few. Migrant ducks arrive in the autumn; the third week in October is often especially important. The Mallard fill the air with their hurrying flight; the pied plumage of the drake Tufted and the rich chocolate and silver of the Pochard add colour to the placid grey of the water. Numbers usually reach a peak in November and December and then, depending on the timing of the onset of wintry weather, decline as they seek ice-free waters. Even in severe weather, however, there are open pools which the ducks themselves help to keep open by swimming around. The Mallard often stand on the ice in large groups and their brilliant orange legs and feet show up vividly. The spring migration may bring a temporary increase of numbers again before the ducks fly away to their breeding grounds and only handfuls of summering birds remain.

Canada Goose on nest in Windsor Great Park.

One of the most evocative sounds of Virginia Water is that of the Canada Geese, the clear bugling call as a skein, V-shaped, in single file or sometimes in a wavy oblique line, flies over the lake. Very often they pass over and on to one of the other waters of the neighbourhood, for they seem to have

67

a preference for the quieter places. They like many of the private estates with their ornamental lakes such as Ascot Place and Sunninghill Park. Even in the Park itself there are often more at the 'Village Pond', the 'Isle of Wight' Pond to give it its proper name, than on the larger waters of the Park and in the moulting season in late summer the neighbouring fields are white with their discarded feathers. If, however, they do decide to stay at Virginia Water, they descend with a crescendo of trumpeting to subside into a comparative silence broken only by a running murmur of cackles as they touch down on the lake.

The Canada Geese, like the Mandarin, are feral. In fact their dependence upon man is much more pronounced. Their typical habitat is that of the man-made environment of parkland and gravel pits rather than the wild places. Nevertheless they evoke the spirit of the wild as they fly restlessly from field to lake, from lake to field. Their association with Virginia Water may go back to the early days of the lake. They had been present in Charles II's collection of wildfowl in St James Park in London and were widespread in the eighteenth century. John Latham wrote in 1785: 'they are thought a great ornament to the pieces of water in many gentlemen's seats, where they are very familiar and breed freely'.

As with most geese, the sexes appear similar: brown bodies and black necks and heads with a distinctive white cheek patch. In the breeding season they have a preference for nesting on small islands in lakes, ponds and gravel pits. The absence of these at Virginia Water is the chief reason why they seldom nest there. After the period of breeding they come together from a wide area and form flocks several hundred strong. In October 1974 there was a flock of 570 in the Great Park and four years later, in the same month, an even larger one of 656. A large flock like this is a spectacular sight and, if it is disturbed, the geese will take to flight with a rising chorus of trumpeting, clearing the trees around the lake and flying away into the distance until their resonant honking is heard no more. Parties are often seen passing overhead in late summer and early autumn. They may be travelling from lake to lake, but they also spend much time feeding on the stubble in the fields. Farmers, whether in the Park or elsewhere, do not always like their presence, for in season they feed on new-sown grass leys and spring and winter wheat, and various measures such as limited egg-destruction are employed to control their numbers. Sir Eric Savill called them 'gross feeders' and the farmers' interests must of course be respected. The Park, however, would be the poorer without them. The Canada Geese make a contribution to the sights and sounds of the Park which goes a long way towards making up for the absence of the truly wild geese.

Virginia Water has many moods. The seasons come and go and with them the birds. In winter the ducks have pride of place. But in summer most of the ducks have gone and there are times when, apart from Coot, the Great Crested Grebes almost have Virginia Water to themselves.

Not that they are there only in the summer. They are present in lesser or greater numbers throughout the year. Large shallow lakes like Virginia Water are well-suited to their manner of life. Nonetheless the colonisation of the Great Park probably did not take place until the eighties and nineties of the last century. Before that they were subject to widespread persecution in response to the demands of the trade in what was known as 'grebe fur' — the white satin-like feathers of the underparts of the bird. At one time Great Crested Grebes were on the point of extinction in Britain. Protective measures were passed, however, and the Grebe was saved. But it is still possible to go to many parts of Britain today and never set eyes on a Great Crested Grebe, so that we must account ourselves fortunate that it is possible to watch them at such close quarters at Virginia Water.

At the beginning of the year the few Grebes at Virginia Water are still in their winter plumage — grey against the steel-grey of the water and the blue-grey of the sky. In some years, as in 1957, there may be as many as 20 present; in other years none at all. Normally there are few compared with those that congregate on the reservoirs and gravel pits to the east of the Great Park. Numbers, however, soon begin to build up. Breeding birds begin to straggle in from the beginning of

February on, though full strength is not reached until April or even later. There are also passage movements in the spring when the number of birds present may be inflated, such as in the case of the 44 recorded at Virginia Water on 26 March 1959.

It is during this time of movement that the birds are most often seen in flight. They are laboured in taking-off as if this was an unusual exercise, and the pied plumage of the wings is as striking as it is unfamiliar. But the water is the true home of the Grebe. It swims with buoyancy and grace and, when hurried, surges forward with powerful strokes, its neck outstretched and held at an angle. It dives almost vertically, leaving scarcely a ripple. Dives often last as much as half-a-minute and the Grebe can surface a considerable distance away.

Quite early in the year some of the Grebes begin to assume breeding plumage and the dull grey of winter gives way to the rich chestnut of the frill or 'tippet' and the dark ear-tufts, which are longer

Great Crested Grebes at Virginia Water.

in the male than the female. Courtship displays too begin early, sometimes as early as January. February, however, is the month when the displays become more frequent. At Virginia Water, in complete disregard for ducks or gulls which may be nearby, two Grebes will approach each other, elongating their necks, with ear-tufts erected vertically and tippets expanded. With their bills a few inches apart, they start a series of head-shakings, 'like a man nodding dissent'. Eventually one Grebe will break off, perhaps dive and re-appear some yards away. One other variety of courtship display which can sometimes be seen at Virginia Water is the 'necks-on-the-water' display. In this two birds swim side by side with necks outstretched and kinked in such a way as to keep their bills close to the water without the expanded tippet actually touching it.

Feeding and courtship are both important activities, but for much of their time before nesting begins in earnest the Grebes are frequently preening or just resting. The head is then drawn right back into the plumage, but the silky white of the slender neck always shows clearly across the water. In preening the bird will often roll over on one side, displaying its white underparts.

Pairing develops steadily and by April it is sometimes possible to be reasonably certain of the number of pairs at Virginia Water. In some years there have been a number of apparently 'unattached' birds. These often gather off Botany Bay Point, opposite the 'Ruins'. The number of pairs breeding at Virginia Water can remain constant for several successive years. For five years in the 1950s, for example, the number of pairs was seven. It then increased to a peak of 16 in 1961. After the hard winter of 1962-63 the number fell sharply, but a recovery took place and in 1967-68 there were again 12-14 pairs. In recent years there has been a decline. Virginia Water is subject to disturbance from the numbers of people who visit it and more and more Grebes seem to prefer the quiet backwaters of local rivers, including the Thames.

The Grebes at Virginia Water have shown considerable adaptability in the nest sites they have chosen. The lake lacks the extensive reed-beds that are used elsewhere in the Park. Sometimes the nest is set back near the bank in the shelter of overhanging rhododendron bushes, inaccessible except from the water. Sometimes the branches of a tree which has fallen over the water provide the foundation for a nest. Often nests are built up on the water weeds some distance from the bank. The nest itself is a large mass of rush stems, sticks and aquatic herbage. These exposed nests are naturally the most open to disturbance. They have also sometimes suffered as heavy rains have raised the water level and in several years nests have been submerged and deserted from this cause. There are occasional examples too of Coots taking over a Grebe's nest. The normal clutch of eggs is three or four. When newly-laid they are chalky white, but contact with the decomposing herbage soon turns them a dirty yellowish-brown. Incubation lasts about four weeks and both sexes take part. The male and female change over at comparatively short intervals. While one bird is sitting, the other is often patrolling off the reeds. Repairs and additions to the nest go on continually. When the Grebe is disturbed at the nest, it will slip silently away but before doing so will often — but not always — cover the eggs with some of the nest material. This serves a double purpose. Not only are the eggs hidden from the view of any passing crow or other potential marauder, but since the whole nest is a mass of slowly decomposing herbage the warmth is thereby retained.

It is not always easy to be certain when the eggs are hatched, because the young Grebes in the early days spend much time on the backs of their parents and are difficult to see. Occasionally they display their presence by thin piping, or they half-slip, half-tumble off into the water. Then there comes more agitated piping until they catch up with their parent and mount to the warmth and security of the back once more. The coloration of the young is striking, the whole body being striped. As the young grow, they become active and insistently demand to be fed. The parents dive, surface and, amid a crescendo of piping, the young hasten to accept the offered food. The piping of the young grebes is one of the most familiar sounds at Virginia Water in July and August.

Yet there is tragedy too. To watch the Grebes engaging in the activity of nest-building, incubating the eggs and feeding the young, and then to see the number of the young decreasing week by week is a saddening experience. Pike are usually presumed to be chiefly responsible. For example 11 young were present at Virginia Water on 24 July 1955; a month later, on 25 August, only six had survived. This story is repeated to a lesser or greater degree every year. Even with the mortality, however, there are the 'good' years, when breeding success is high. On 4 September 1961 there were still at Virginia Water 26 adults and 22 young. There are times too when a second brood is raised. In 1968 there was a pair with half-grown young as late as 31 October.

The numbers begin to drop off by October, sometimes even earlier. There are almost always, however, some present through November and December. And so the year comes to an end and, with the New Year, another cycle in the life of the Great Crested Grebe begins.

Like a grey statue the heron stands motionless at the water's edge, watching and waiting. Or with measured movements of his broad rounded wings, he flies over Virginia Water itself. He has almost certainly come from the heronry between Fort Belvedere and the lake. The nests are high in Scots pines and sweet chestnuts, adjacent to the Drive which was planted with cedars in the eighteenth century to flank the carriageway which led to Virginia Water.

There have been herons in Windsor Great Park for many centuries; they are no newcomers like the Mandarin Ducks, the Canada Geese and the Great Crested Grebes. And where there were herons there were heronries. The oldest record is that marked on John Norden's *View of the Great Park* of 1607. At this time the 'Hernery' was in the area between Bishopsgate and Snow Hill (where the 'Copper Horse' now is). By the first half of the nineteenth century the herons had moved to the neighbourhood of Sandpit Gate on the western side of the Great Park. Leith Ritchie, writing in the 1840s, talked about 'the herons soaring over the lofty tops of the trees' and spoke of the nests being 'built on beech trees of an enormous height'. The herons eventually moved from this nesting-site soon after the formation of the Windsor Great Park Volunteer Rifle Corps in 1859. William Menzies, author of *Windsor Park and Forest*, made the comment: 'These birds love solitude, and were disturbed by the rifle practice at the Ranges close by the Gate where they had occupied some large trees from earliest times'.

He recorded that the new heronry was near the Fishing Cottage at Virginia Water. Whenever the move took place, it created an association with Virginia Water which, although the precise location of the heronry changed from time to time, has lasted to the present day. From the northern side the heronry at some unrecorded date transferred to the south side of the lake. By 1948 the heronry had moved to the grounds of Fort Belvedere and there it has remained. The site is an excellent one for herons. It is secluded and subject to a minimum of disturbance. And yet it is within a few hundred yards of Virginia Water, which has all the facilities for early morning fishing exucursions.

Herons nest at Fort Belvedere early in the year. They are often back in the vicinity of the heronry by February and breeding is always in full swing by April. Even more than most birds they are in consequence dependent on the weather conditions. A cold wet spring, with high winds, can have disastrous effects, for the nests are high and exposed to the elements. The lowest nests are about 60 feet above ground level and the highest sometimes over 100 feet. The nests are untidy bulky structures of sticks and weeds, lined with rushes, wool and other soft materials. Sometimes two nests will be virtually joined together, though perhaps only one is in use and the second will serve as a reserve supply of nesting material.

Most of the trees in which the heronry is built are now well over 200 years old and in recent years many high boughs have fallen from them. The section of the belt of trees in which the nests are situated is at the most about a quarter of a mile in length. The herons have always kept to this small, clearly defined area. When the birds first started building at this site, they mainly favoured the Scots pines for their nests. It is only since about 1970 that they have been making more and more use of the sweet chestnuts. Certain trees are favoured for nesting within the colony. One Scots pine for many years regularly had six or more nests in it and as many as 14 in 1954. This was the year when, with 70 nests, the heronry was one of the largest in Britain. Weather conditions were exceptionally good — no high winds or unseasonable snowstorms as in many years and no signs either of nests blown down or of dead fledglings. Since then the fortunes of the heronry have fluctuated. In the years following the severe winter of 1962-63 the number of nests fell to 20 or less and it has only been in the last few years that the numbers have approached the high level of the early fifties. In 1978 the number reached 50 for the first time since 1956 and, after a decline following the hard weather of the early months of 1979, in 1980, with its long dry and mild spring, the total reached 52.

Not only were there more nests in 1980 than for many years; there were so many young in the nests that there was apparently not enough room for all of them and some fell or were pushed out. In a good breeding year, once the young are hatched the heronry becomes a scene of activity in which the weakest go to the wall. The young become voraciously hungry and, when they are old enough, stand erect on the nests. The parent birds come and go frequently, and each time one of the herons with well-filled gullet is seen sweeping downwards, the young birds in the whole group of nests are thrown into a state of great excitement. There is a storm of extraordinary sounds — grunts, squeals, screams, chatterings and barkings like a persistent hammering. When the parent bird has settled on its own nest and fed its young, which it does by regurgitating its food, the sounds die away, until with the approach of another adult the vocal tempest rages among the tree tops all over again. Sometimes ten or more of the herons are over the trees at the same time — a majestic sight.

By June the young have learnt to fly and one by one leave the nests. The adults depart too until the heronry is deserted. Some may go right away. There is no true migration with herons, but there can be a dispersal over a wide area. Some of the Fort Belvedere herons, however, probably remain in the neighbourhood, for both at Virginia Water and the other lakes of the Park there are few times of the year when there are none to be seen. Sometimes four or five stand or perch together — perhaps these are the young of the year — but for the most part herons seem to be 'loners', content with their own company until the new year comes round, and their social and gregarious instincts revive and they return to the traditional heronry for a new breeding season.

Apart from the four 'special' birds of Virginia Water — the Mandarin ducks, the Canada Geese, the Great Crested Grebes and the Herons, there are many more to be seen and heard both on the lake itself and in the surrounding woodlands. They are there for those who visit Virginia Water to discover and to enjoy — the hawfinches high in the hornbeams; winter visitors like the siskins and redpolls which are attracted by the alders; the fieldfares and redwings which join with the resident mistle thrushes to feed on the berry-bearing shrubs and trees of the Heather Garden; the grey wagtails as much at home among the tumbling waters of the Cascade as if it were a Welsh waterfall; the slate-blue nuthatches and the mousey tree-creepers that move secretively among the trees . . . Virginia Water is a paradise for birds.

Key to Caption Credits

The illustrations from the Royal Library
(RL) are reproduced by gracious permission
of Her Majesty The Queen.
BT   Barbara Thompson
GL   Gordon Langsbury
RS   Ray South
V & A   Victoria and Albert Museum

Note on Sources

In addition to the Crown Estate records in the Public Record Office, the Royal Archives in Windsor Castle and other records referred to, many diaries and memoirs have been used. Among them are those of Mrs Delany, Horace Walpole and John Cam Hobhouse.

The most important nineteenth century books on Windsor Great Park are those of W. Menzies, *Windsor Great Park and Forest* (1864) and G.M. Hughes, *A History of Windsor Forest, Sunninghill and the Great Park* (1890). R.J. Elliott's *The Story of Windsor Great Park* is a recent account. Sir Owen Morshead's *George IV and Royal Lodge* is an enjoyable monograph. The article by G.E. Chambers on *The Ruins at Virginia Water* is in the *Berks Archaeological Journal*, vol 54 and there is a more recent article on *Windsor Great Park* by M. Binney in *Country Life* for 30 July 1981.

The Phaidon volume of Thomas and Paul Sandby's *Drawings . . . at Windsor Castle* gives details of many of their illustrations of the Park. J. Hakewill's *The History of Windsor and its Neighbourhood* was originally published in 1813, but later editions contained *Illustrations of Virginia Water and the Adjacent Scenery* drawn by W.A. Delamotte jnr in the 1820s.

For the last two chapters, L. Roper's *The Gardens in the Great Park* (1959) contains an account of the early years of the Valley Garden. C. Savage wrote a monograph on *The Mandarin Duck* in 1952, which has never been superseded. *Great Crested Grebes in Windsor Park* by the present author appeared in *The Middle Thames Naturalist* for 1965 and he also collaborated with J.R. and T.M. Chappell in an article on *A Royal Heronry* in the *Surrey Bird Report* for 1978.

References

PRO	Public Record Office
RA	Royal Archives, Windsor
CP	Cumberland Papers
QVJ	Queen Victoria's Journal
PP	Privy Purse Papers
Greville	The Greville Memoirs ed Roger Fulford 1963
Huish	Memoirs of George IV 1830

Before the Lake
1 Pepys, Diary 19 Aug 1665
2 Hughes, History of Windsor Forest p294

A Great Ornament
1 Pote, History & Antiquities of Windsor Castle pp20-1
2 Pote, Delices de Windsore pp74-5
3 RA CP 70/1-10, 24, 143
4 Thompson E.P., Whigs and Hunters,   p41
5 RA CP 70/161
6 Knight, C (snr), Windsor Guide 1793, pp99-100

The Royal Renewal
1 Knight, C (jnr), Passages of a Working Life, I 37-8
2 Pitt's Estate Act, 1782. 22 Geo III, no 22
3 PRO CRES 2/57
4 ibid   19 May 1788
5 ibid   11 Aug 1789
6 ibid   15 Dec 1788
7 ibid   15 Dec 1788
8 ibid   20 Sept 1789
8 ibid   15 Jan 1789
10 ibid   4 Feb 1789
11 ibid   28 Aug 1807
12 ibid   10 Oct 1790
13 ibid   6 Oct 1788
14 ibid   20 Sept 1789

Prinny's Gilded Toy
1 Huish II 247
2 Rural Rides, Everyman ed I 125
3 Huish II 53
4 PRO CRES 2/57. 23 Oct 1815, 30 Aug 1824, 7 June 1828, 4 March 1830
5 Greville p48
6 Huish II 361
7 Greville p48
8 Creevy Papers II 233
9 Chambers G.E., Berks 'Arch, Journal LIV 39-52

10 Knight C (jnr) Journey Book of Berkshire p62
11 Jesse, E A Summer's Day at Windsor 1841 p117
12 Ritchie, L Windsor Castle and its Environs 1848 p287

Their Majesties' Pleasure
1 Greville op cit p45
2 ibid   pp48-9
3 Letters of Queen Victoria. First Series I 16-17
4 RA QVJ 4 June 1851
5 ibid   12 Sept 1837
6 ibid   19 Sept 1837
7 ibid   29 Sept 1837
8 ibid   30 Aug 1838
9 ibid   12 Sept 1838
10 ibid   15 Sept 1838
11 ibid   13 June 1839
12 ibid   17 Aug 1839
13 ibid   11 Oct 1844
14 ibid   8-9 Sept 1838
15 ibid   10 Feb 1851
16 ibid   18 Aug 1841
17 ibid   17 Aug 1842
18 ibid   26 Aug 1843
19 ibid   5 July 1853
20 ibid   16,17 Jan 1861
21 RA PP Windsor 1510
22 ibid   367
23 RA GV PP Windsor 9
24 RA GV Diary 18 June 1905, 23 June 1907
25 RA PP Windsor 1235, 1236, 1238
26 ibid 379, 380, 387, 388, 408-10, 447
27 RA GV PP Windsor 1817
28 RA PP Windsor 851
29 ibid   1046-50
30 ibid   850
31 ibid   884
32 ibid   884
33 ibid   885
34 ibid   967
35 ibid   1660
36 ibid 1558
37 ibid   1581
38 ibid   1035
39 RA GV PP Windsor 213
40 ibid 192
41 ibid   388
42 ibid   1817
43 ibid   1817

Index

Subscribers

Presentation Copies

1 Her Majesty The Queen
2 HRH The Prince Philip, Duke of Edinburgh, Ranger
3 A.R. Wiseman, Deputy Ranger
4 John Bond, Keeper of the Queen's Gardens
5 Windsor Library
6 Slough Library
7 Maidenhead Library

8 Raymond South	56 Daphne V. Fido	103 David Jefferson	150 Marian Griffin
9 Clive & Carolyn Birch	57 Mrs Angela Perkins	104 Ernest A. Day MVO	151 Rosemary & Michael Burstall
10 Rev John E. Hirst	58 D.R. Garrett	105 Arthur J. Wells	152 Barbara & David Cass-Beggs
11 Roland Paul Snelling	59	106 Mrs J.R. Waltham	153 Joan Cass
12 Mrs Anna Ross	60 Reg Stevenson	107 M.J. Waltham	154 Helen & Howard Davies
13 Percy G. Higgs	61 G.H.S. Toller	108 Mrs C.M. Denby	155 Anthony John Parnell
14 Mary Stella Graham	62 Ian M. Leishman	109 Joe & Ruth Newman	156 Gordon Cullingham
15 M.F. Bond	63 Royal Free Middle School	110 A.W. Sampson	157
16 Derek McCulloch	64 R. South	111 J.C. Sampson	158 David C. Hedges
17 T.W. Smith	65	112 P.W. Sampson	159 Gordon Langsbury FRPS
18 Mrs J.E. Pearce	66 Mulle Price	113 G. Dootson	160 Sheila Wallace
19 Upton House School	67 Alan W. Fone	114 Miss B.M. Smith	161 John A. Meredith
20 Anthony J. Hutchings	68 Harry Hubbard	115 Dr D.K.M. Thomas	162 N.M. Waring
21 D. & M. Dennis	69 K. Buckingham	116 Gladys Reeves	163 Mrs M.L. Martin
22 Rev Denis Shaw	70 Dr C.J. Buckingham	117 Mrs Jean Kirkwood	164 D.J. Poynter
23	71 E.E. Green	118 Alan Gillies	165 K. Domellof
24 Mrs Joan Davis	72 D.D. Hartridge	119 J.H.A. Gibson TD	166 John Counsell
25 L.E. Wells	73 C.A. Hill	120 Mrs Muriel Stillwell	167 Cecily M. Adcock
26 Mrs Mary Fountain	74 Irene M. Aylett	121 Clifford & Dorothy Howard	168 A.C. Fraser
27 Pamela M. Boseley	75 Martin Albertini	122 Patrick Purchase	169 John Crump
28 Mrs L.M. Whittome	76 Lt Col R.J. Wyatt MBE TD	123 Peter John Finch	170 Mrs Alice Anne Pack
29	77 Dr F. John Long	124 Isobel Mary Baker	171 R.L. Bull
30 Heatherwood & Windsor Park	78 Terence Emery	125 Dorothy Johnston	172 Elizabeth Brown
32 GMWU	79 Margaret Jean Curtis	126 Marjorie E. South	173 F.J. Alderman
33 Irene M. Aylett	80 J.M. Pinder	127 Joan George	174 Mrs Caroline Lewis
34 E.H. Cuthbert	81 Jon Nickerson	128 John Newman	175 Ronald Edwards
35 C.J. Howlett	82 J.T. Clarke	129 Gillian Newman	176 G.B. Warner
36 Peter Chard	83 Patricia M.H. Roach	130 Ruth Whitelaw	177 T.W. Taylor MVO OBE
37 John B. Dyson	84 Florence Meech	131 Bridget Whitelaw	178 Mr & Mrs E.K. Rodbard-Brown
38 Mrs S. Angell	85 D. Barnard	132 Barbara Thompson	179 Mrs B.M. Douglas-Hamilton
39 Victoria & Albert Museum	86 P.D. Barnard	133 Daphne Fido	180 Mrs Naomi Jackson
40 J.H. Sand	87 Fred Price	134 Brenda Williamson	181 John Counsell
41 Mrs I. Hollis	88 M.J. Stanier	135 Lavender Whittome	182 R.G. Beck
42 Melva Wood	89 Desmond & Joy Saunders	136 Derek R. Waters	183
43 F.W. Jones	90 J.H. Flint	137 Dr H.W. Parris	184 Mrs Ida Baker
44 G.S. Parker	91 Dr S.I. Lewis	138	185 Mrs Hilary Brooks
45 S.W.B. Watson	92 Anwen Jones	139 Doris Charlish	186 Geoffrey Hawthorn
46 Mrs S.M. Le Vesconte	93 Joye Beckett	140 Jill Moulton	187 Eric C. Crowe
47 Miss Jane Langton	94 Mrs H.L. Hedges	141 Mrs A.W.G. McQueen	188 Miss Hilda Hamblin
48 Peter Ellis Jones	95 Joan Spurgeon	142 J.E. Handcock	189 Audrey Sinclair
49 Mrs J.M. Timms	96 S.W. Treadgold	143 A.G. Brown	190 John A. Chappell
50 Grace Stephen	97 T.J. Greenaway	144 Lillie F. South	191 Mrs J.H.M. Weston
51 Edward Whiteley	98 J.C. & F.M.R. Newman	145 Peter Harrison	192 Ralph & Alwena Maddern
52 V.S. Stoner	99 Dr E.C. Willatts OBE	146 Ian Walker	193 J.P. Manley
53 Mrs P.M. Hockedy	100 Brian Wickham Atkinson	147 Bruce Denney	194 K.G. Wheatley
54 Cllr Denis J. Downham	101 A.E. & D.E. De'Ath	148 Roger Denney	195 Len & Joan Critchlow
55 Bishop Woods	102 J.F. Hoppe	149 Ann Thompson	196

197 R.W. Portus
198 Miss Mary Corfield
199 Mrs Jean Meikle Palmer
200 Harold Basford
201 Mary Clayden
202 Dorothy Sparks
203 R.N. McRae
204 Daphne Moseley
205 Angela Feldstein
206 Ruth Manwaring
207 Joan Madge
208 Carol Male
209 F.J. Cassie
210 Kate Hobbs
211 Mrs K.A. Manger MBE
212 L.E.V. Butler
213 The Librarian, Nature
    Conservancy Council
214 C.J. Gilson
215 Audrey M. Probart
216 H.E. Pashley
217 David Willmott
218 Mrs D.H. Grove
219 D.B. Eastwood
220 J.K. Letts
221 Doreen E. Gibbons
222 K.D. King
223 Mrs Margaret Whitelaw
224
225 Miss C.E. Brettell
226 Mrs A. Knight
227 Ann Timperley
228 Nature Conservancy Council
229 Bessie E. Crook
230 Mrs Judith Hunter
231 Windsor Boys' School
232 P.A. Blake

233 S.J.R. Rumsey
234
235 L. Ross
236 S.C. Brown
237
238 Allan Hale
239 Colin E. Dean
240 The Royal Library
241 Mrs R.P. Harbron
242 E.G. Perry
243 Barbara Ann Story
244 R.J. Elliott
245 Ian H. Plested
246 A.L. Forster
247 Mrs Margaret Holland
248 Peter G. Kingswood
249 J.W. Salway
250 A.E. Villiers
251 Heather Hunter
252 Richard Cox
253 Mrs Muriel Bookless
254 D. Rob't Harman
255 Peter Hjul
256 S.A. Oliver
257 A.L. Oliver
258 K.A. Nalder
259 Mrs B. Whalley
260 Mrs Denis Tunnicliffe
261
262 Dr Malcolm Deane
263 W. Horder
264 Graham Jones Rankin
265
266 R.M. Brown
267
268 Nicol Mutch
269 Malcolm Collier

270 C.B. Gilbert
271 Mrs R. St. John
272 Peter Anthony Blake
273 The Windsor Boys' School
274 J.G. Thomas
275 R. Munns BA ALA
276 P.L. Buet
277 Mrs L. Parkes
278 The Princess Margaret
279 Royal Free School
280 R.G. & A.C. Beauchamp
281 Mrs I.E. Tourlamain
282 Mrs P. Bennett
283 Vera M. Hopkins
284
285 Mrs D. Hills
286 Miss V.C. McIntosh
287 Mr & Mrs R.A. Barber
288 V.M. Bairstow
289 Mr & Mrs R.G. Davis
290 David L. Sawtell
291 Nicola Brooker
292 Sally Rosenthal
293 Carole Davies
294 Helen McTiffin
295 Alan & Gillian Massey
296 Maureen Plumridge
297 P. Dennis
298 J. Fry
299 Miss Barbara Bassil
300 Leslie Grout
301 H.C. Macey
302 Andrew Shaw
303 Peter Gray
304 C.R. Anderson
305 Mrs D.M. Shakespeare
306 G.A. McDermott

307 Miss K.M. Shawcross
308
309 Mrs O.E. White
310 Mrs Bridget Smith
311 Wm A. Phillips
312 P.G. Dunnington
313 J. Dunnington
314 Paul & Linda Ayres
315 Mrs Olive Gosling
316 Mrs Vera Cook
317 A.C. Kelsey
318 K.M. Bigsby
319 Mrs Pat Thomas
320 Mrs D. Burley
321 Miss F.M. Reed
323 D.M.J. Higgs
324 Mrs J. Waterfield
325 R. Corry
326 Mrs V. Bonham
327 Ian & Carys Maxwell
328 George Jasieniecki
329 E.A. Bennett
330 Col R.O. Mells
331 G. Howe
332 Miss E. Lewis
333 S.G. Spelman
334 Mrs M.E. Lewis
335
350 Surrey County Library
351 Mrs M.C. Pearmund
352 Mrs E. Desborough
353 Mrs Anne Taylor
354 Charles E. Bray

Remaining names unlisted